TOTON

A collection of memories, photographs, & research

Postcard circa 1963

During a chance conversation with an unknown gentleman, he asked us to include in the Nottinghamshire Countryside a few notes on the history of Toton. This gentleman's request cannot easily be complied with, although it is not because Toton has no history as probably there is a good deal but unfortunately the known records are scanty. – J Bramley Nottinghamshire Countryside magazine 1948.

This book aims to correct this statement.

Many historical records do exist, they are just scattered. Photographs, maps, postcards and other material are available in personal albums, archives and libraries. Memories add mental 'pictures' of the social life, characters and events that have all been involved with the development of Toton, a township in the Parish of Attenborough.

Rex Wyatt and Gillian Morral

By the range of the historical period covered, and the number of people, who have at one time or another lived in Toton, there is a wealth of source material. In an effort not to overwhelm the reader, there must of necessity be omissions. I wish I could include all the anecdotes, events and photographs but the book would be huge.

Whilst every care has been taken to ensure the accuracy of the information contained in this book, the authors cannot accept responsibility for any error or omission. Contrasting opinions and description of events have been encountered and a fair balance has been aimed for. This book has been written with every good intention, to put Toton on the "map", to note the changes that have taken place and understand our area a little more.

The words in italics are quotations from texts given to Rex Wyatt and myself and collected over many years from local residents and others, connected to this unique township.

Dedication

I would like to dedicate this book to all the people of Toton.

Published by G.E. Morral 2012

Printed by Russell Press Ltd. Russell House, Bulwell Lane, Basford, Nottingham NG6 0BT

Tel 0115 9784505

ISBN 978-0-957 4853-0-3

Authors' Notes

I have lived in Toton nearly all of my life, being brought up in Chetwynd Road and moving to Portland Road forty years ago. At the back of my home was a mill pond (now filled in) so when I retired from business in Nottingham, I decided to investigate where the mill once stood.

I have had help from many local people and I would like to thank them all. My first contact was Alan Lewis, then with a young man Michael Harvey who was about to go to University to study photography. Without his expertise a lot of my photographs would not be possible because many of them came from a battered small black and white Brownie camera and some photographs were just one inch square. Eileen Hall and Norman Lewis, with their great knowledge of Toton, have been very helpful, providing many of the photographs and information.

Rex Wyatt

Retirement seems to be the time to take up new hobbies and learn new tricks! Researching the history of Toton, learning to read writing of 17th century folk and talking to many interesting people has been my experience of retirement.

Toton is a little known part of Nottinghamshire but there is a wealth of information tucked out of sight. Visits to Chester and Nottingham, to archives, libraries and museums have been just part of this study into Toton, its life and history. Discussion with museum curators has been informative. Talks with many Toton people has been fascinating and I would like to pay tribute to all those who have shared their memories, their expertise and given or lent old photographs.

Gillian E Morral

Acknowledgements

Rex and I would like to thank the many people, who have unstintingly given their time, lent their photographs and described their memories. In particular we would like to thank Eileen Hall, Norman Lewis, Susan Wilkinson, Michael Harvey, Stan Leighton, Tony Taylor, and all the other Toton and Attenborough residents, with whom we have talked.

Thanks must also go to the staff at various libraries, especially to the staff at Nottinghamshire and Chester Archives, for their help in finding documents and deciphering some of the language. Thanks must also go to friends and family for their patience and for helping clarify ideas, through discussion and comment, in particular Christine Hibbert, Jessie Lemons and my husband John.

Aerial View of Toton 1976

Bispham Drive
Junior School

Other Side
of the Moon

Chambers
Packaging

Chilwell Ordnance Depot

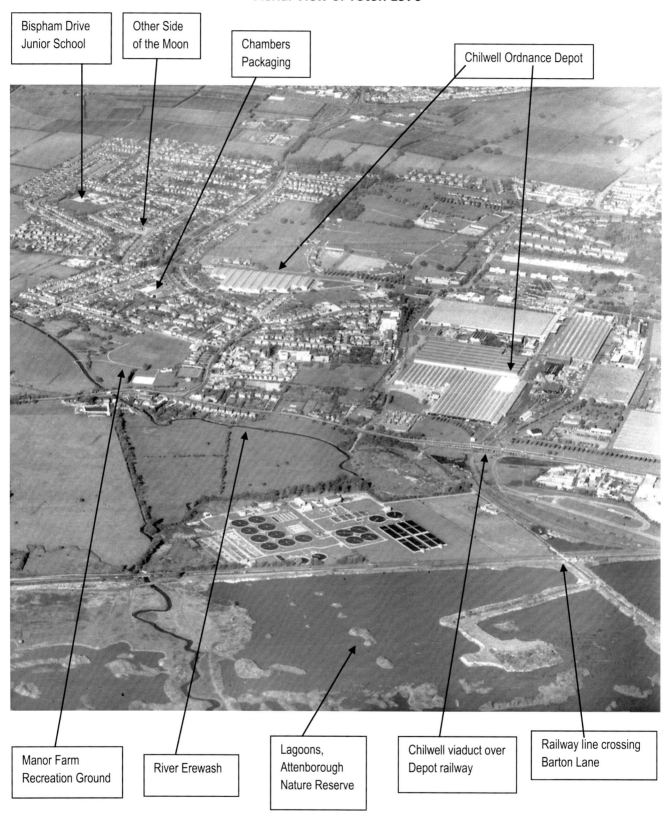

Manor Farm
Recreation Ground

River Erewash

Lagoons,
Attenborough
Nature Reserve

Chilwell viaduct over
Depot railway

Railway line crossing
Barton Lane

Photograph courtesy M.O.D. Chilwell Station

Early Toton

Geese were a prominent feature of farming life in past centuries, used for food and feathers and sold at markets and fairs such as Nottingham's Goose Fair.

Contents page

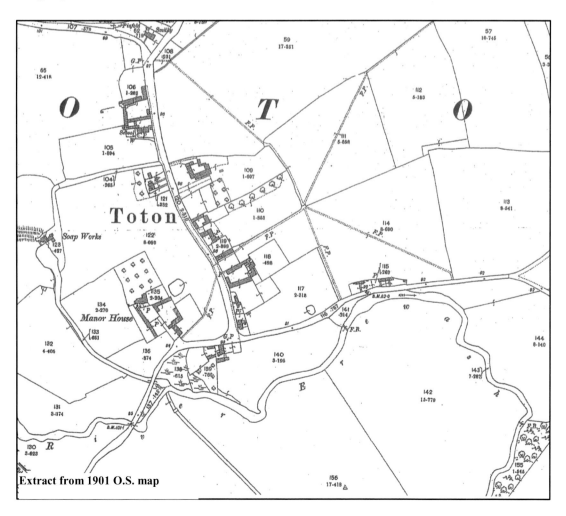

Extract from 1901 O.S. map

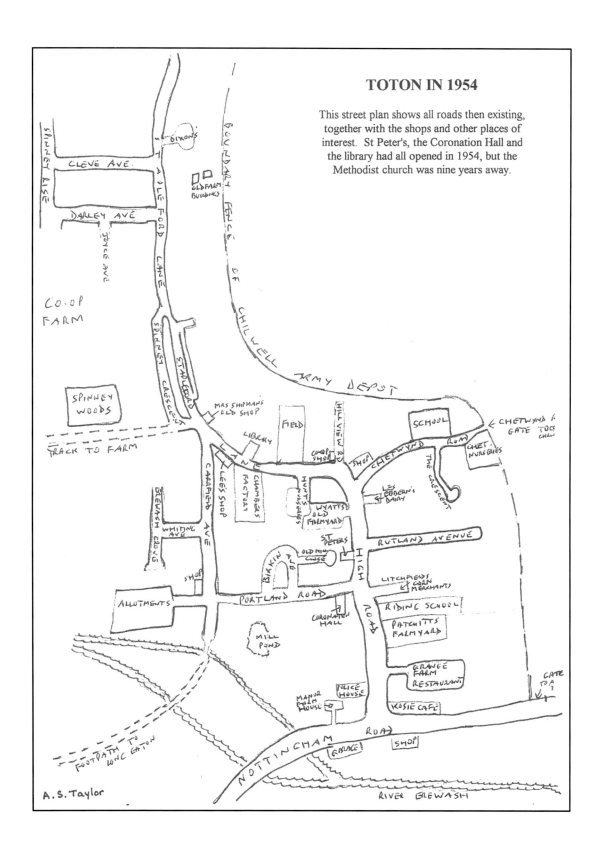

TOTON IN 1954

This street plan shows all roads then existing, together with the shops and other places of interest. St Peter's, the Coronation Hall and the library had all opened in 1954, but the Methodist church was nine years away.

Drawn from memory A.S.Taylor

TOTON

Toton today is a pleasant residential area in the south-west corner of Nottinghamshire. It is bounded by the Rivers Trent and Erewash on the south and west and the Parishes of Attenborough, Chilwell and Stapleford to the east and north.

Aerial view Toton north

Besides the numerous houses, which cover a large part of the land now, there are three schools, three churches, two community halls, two small shops and several small businesses including hairdressers and pubs and the not so small Toton Railway Sidings. Indeed this was once one of the largest marshalling yards in Europe and certainly brought people into Toton to live. Nowadays people are able to commute to Nottingham, Derby and Leicester because of the available transport links. The Motorway M1 is close by and a good bus service runs frequently between Long Eaton and Nottingham.

The largest employer is the, much loved or hated, superstore Tesco with the nearby Chetwynd Barracks across the road a close second. Nearby is the successful Nottingham University and the busy town of Beeston with several large employers such as Boots and the Royal Mail.

Small open areas are available for leisure and recreation with play areas for children, sports areas and open land for dog walkers. There is a local nature reserve and pleasant areas for walking especially at the nearby Attenborough Nature Reserve.

Aerial view Toton centre 1987

Site Mill Pond   Portland Rd   Douglas Court

Within this peaceful 'suburb' of Chilwell and Beeston, are various social and charitable groups which meet on a regular basis. Toton is a thriving and unique place.

In Days Gone by

In days gone by Toton was not so populous; indeed one survey records just nine houses. Toton is, however, an ancient place. It had half a church, which was St Mary's in Attenborough, the other half of this church being in the Manor of Chilwell. Toton, a Township in the Parish of Attenborough, has been recorded as Tovetune and Tolvestune and later as Tawton. Its name existed before 1066, possibly being derived from the personal name "Torolf" and "tun" meaning farmstead. It finally became Toton in the 17th century.

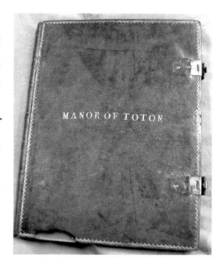

Rent book of Toton in Nottinghamshire Archives

Prior to 1066 Aldene the Saxon owned the land. Following the successful Norman Invasion, William the Conqueror granted the land, along with large parts of six counties to William Peverill. This eminent Lord was given many manors and so began the long pattern of absentee landlords and tenant farmers.

The entry for Toton in the Domesday Book, compiled in 1086 for taxation purposes, records that Warner was the chief tenant or manager. Under him were four sochmen (sokemen) or ordinary tenants. These were freemen who paid a monetary rent and below them were sixteen villeins who worked on Warner's land rather than pay rent. This was the time when medieval strip farming was practised, with the number of strips per person reflecting their status in the village. The lowest rank of villagers, were bordars[1] of whom there were three recorded. The Manor of Toton is stated as covering three carucates or about 360 acres,[2] with a population of twenty four households. There were two mills, a hundred acres of meadow lands and a plantation of willows.[3] There was half a church and a priest at this time.

In Towertune is Aldene 3 carucates of land to the geld. (There is) land for 3 ½ ploughs. There Warner, William's man, has 3 ploughs and 4 sokemen on 3 bovates of this land 16 villeins and 3 bordars having 6 ploughs. There is half a church and a priest and 2 mills (rendering) 8 s(shillings) and 100 acres of meadow and a little plantation of willows. Tre[4] as now it was worth 60s.

extract from Domesday book online

Ralph Fitzhubert, another Norman nobleman, had land in Chilwell which included 5 bovates (the area that could be cultivated by a plough drawn by one ox in the annual ploughing season) of sokeland belonging to Toton.

---

[1] Bordar – a cottager

[2] Caracutes - amount of land that could be tilled by eight oxen, about 360 acres

[3] Then and Now online

[4] Tre - village

During the centuries that followed, the Manor of Toton passed to the Grey family via a marriage in 1208 of Isolda (Warner?) daughter of Robert of Toton, to Henry de Grey. The de Greys were powerful figures in Nottinghamshire; Lord John de Grey in the 1270s was Sheriff of Nottinghamshire and Derbyshire and Governor of Nottingham Castle. Their seat was Codnor Castle, an important castle in medieval times. At this time the population of Toton had not changed a great deal. There were still four freeholders and a number of villeins or bondmen. By now, there was a dovecote but it cannot have been a very grand affair as it was worth nothing! The Manor now had a garden and there was still land for ploughing, meadow land and two mills. In 1308, only one mill is mentioned. This was a watermill and would probably have been sited on the River Erewash in the current Manor Park. Toton Manor was "*a capital messuage[5] worth yearly 3s 4d. There are 60 acres of meadow worth yearly 53s price of the acre 2s 8d.*" [6] By now, there were six freemen, one of whom was Richard le Daye. The Day family feature throughout the centuries and indeed play a valuable part in the life of the Manor and in Attenborough in particular. Another freeman, Roger Blale or Blake had descendents still in Toton some three hundred years later. He held one messuage 1½ oxgangs of land and paid 20s rent twice a year. Besides the freemen, there were six bondsmen and five cotters. The bondsmen each held a toft[7] and two oxgangs[8] of land and paid a monetary rent. The land beside their house would be used for growing vegetables such as beans. The cotters were the poorest people in the village. Their houses would have been close to the Manor House, with the workers walking to the strips of land to plough and maintain the land.

> *And the garden of the said Manor is worth yearly 6s 8d And there is a new dovehouse worth nothing And he holds in his demesne there 16 oxgangs of land whereof each contains 9 acres and each oxgang is worth yearly 5s sum £4*
>
> *4 freeholders who hold 11 oxgangs of land and render yearly 11s 6d doing suit of court every 3 weeks*
>
> *There are 2 mills which are worth yearly £4 Bondmen (bondii) who hold 37 oxgangs of land with a park wherein each oxgang is worth yearly 5s with the works of the bondmen sum £9 5s 0d*
>
> *And there is pasture to the said manor which is worth yearly £5*
>
> *And perquisities of court worth yearly 5s 8d*
>
> *And they say that the advowson of the church of Adinbur belongs to the said Manor which is worth yearly 20 marcs*
>
> 1271 Inquisitions & Post Mortems - Nottinghamshire Thoroton

The men of Toton also served in the army, when required. Fifteen archers are recorded as fit to serve in 1539. Some thirty years earlier in 1506, in the reign of Henry VII one archer and some billmen (who used billhooks[9]) served with Francis Lovell.

When the Order of the Garter was founded in 1348 by Edward III, a Lord John Grey was made a Knight of this prestigious group, as was his grandson Richard, indicating the high esteem in which the King held them. The Greys held Toton from 1208 until 1561, when Elizabeth I granted the Manor of Toton to Richard Whalley of Screveton (via another advantageous marriage). Whalley unfortunately backed the wrong side during the reign of

---

[5] Messuage - dwelling house, adjacent buildings, garden, orchard and land connected to the house

[6] Thoroton Vol ll Inquisitions

[7] Toft - land on which a peasant's house and outbuildings stood.

[8] Oxgang - measure of land area cultivated by a plough drawn by one ox in one year.

[9] Billhook - A pole with a bill-like blade mounted below a spearhead with spikes added and used in battle and on farms

Edward VI and was fined and subsequently struggled to maintain his position in the county. Richard Whalley took out a massive loan from Sir Thomas Stanhope and when Whalley defaulted on the conditions of the loan in 1571, Sir Thomas acquired the Manor.

The Stanhopes were another family with great local power; they owned Elvaston Castle in Derbyshire, a substantial manor house at Shelford and other manors in Nottinghamshire. They saw great changes during their hundred years of owning Toton Manor. The Reformation came to England and the political powers changed, as the monarchs changed. However life for most people still carried on regardless, the land was farmed, the rivers fished and rents were paid. It appears to be at this time purely a monetary rent, the medieval practice of payment in kind having died out. The large landowners like Sir Thomas and then Sir John Stanhope must have found this a lucrative business, as the income from Toton Manor itself was quite substantial. Dues were collected at Toton Manor House where there was a court. Indeed it was at this court in 1603 that the oath of Allegiance to King James I was sworn. George Attenborough, Thomas Commyn, John Smalley, Richard Blake and William Johnson are among those who are recorded as taking the oath.

Court book of Toton Manor

Some years later in 1612, William Johnson and Frances Johnson were reprimanded for not attending divine service on Sunday 27th. The reason: they were dancing. Perhaps this is a record of Morris dancing. William Johnson was one of the better-off tenants. His rental for 1620/1621 was twenty shillings, compared with Richard Blake (four pence) and George Wood (eight shillings). Francis Cooke seems to be the wealthiest tenant, at this time.[1]

George Jaques rented land and kept accurate accounts for Sir John Stanhope. For this, he appears to have received a wage about £22 a year. During the first half of the seventeenth century there were fifteen people renting pieces of land paying rents between £5 and £30 a half year for different qualities of

Notes written by Sir John Stanhope, in the rent book 1628

---

[1] Toton Rent book 1620 -21 DD39/4

11

land (see Appendix 1). Eight others, only rented cottages, in Toton, so one supposes that these were labourers, the cottars mentioned in earlier records.

The English Civil War (1642-1646) interrupted the peaceful life of the country. Henry Ireton, from Attenborough village took a leading role in the ensuing battles. However, in Toton itself, life did not change a great deal; the rent was still collected at the same time and from the same tenants. The aftermath of the Civil War brought forfeits and fines from the victorious Parliamentarians. A court case ensued in which the surviving son of Sir John Stanhope had to prove that Toton estate passed to him, not to his stepfather Sir John Gell, a Royalist[11]. However this must have taken time and money as the said inheritor, John Stanhope, had to mortgage the land to raise money, presumably to pay for the court case and possibly help pay his stepfather's fines.

Arthur Warren stepped into the situation and bought the estate off Sir John. Arthur Warren, (born in Thorpe Arnold in Leicestershire 1617), worked in Gray's Inn, London, presumably as a lawyer. He bought Toton Manor around 1660 as a retirement home. He did not move in to the Manor House until just before he died. He, however, did accrue the lucrative rents from the thirty-three or so tenants, plus the rents from the Chilwell men. In 1670 the total income was £224 and 4 shillings which must have been a considerable sum for the period.

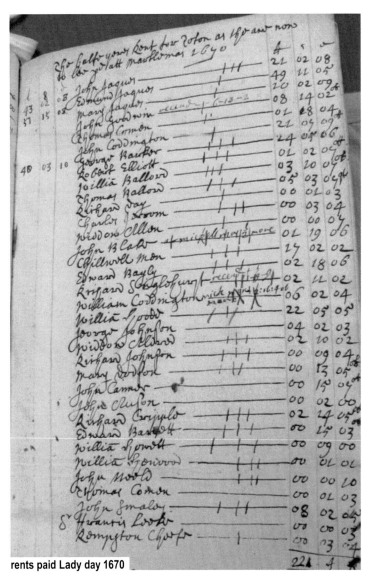

rents paid Lady day 1670

He was, perhaps, what we would call today a financial wheeler dealer. He stood surety for a charity to help victims of a disastrous fire in 1694 in Long Eaton[12] and was a trustee for the winding up of the Palmes estate in Stapleford. This enabled him to help his son, also Arthur Warren, to purchase Stapleford Hall. 1676 saw the transfer of Toton Estate with all the fishing rights and tenants to Arthur Warren junior, with the land in trust for his descendents.

---

[11] Lady Mary Stanhope married Sir John Gell on the death of her husband. Her son John Stanhope inherited Toton.

[12] Long Eaton and Sawley Archives online

Whilst the ownership of the land changed, the families who lived in Toton remained constant. The Cummings(Comynn) Chambers, Johnsons, Smalleys, and Jaques feature in all the 17th century rent books. They worked on various lands in Toton such as Mucklemore Close, Stone Meadow, Swan Nest or in the Teathering Leas, Great Eastfield or Trent Close. Rent was paid twice yearly.

Toton (with Attenborough) had about eleven houses during this period. Most were small affairs with only one chimney. They would have been long narrow houses with a central hearth. The unpopular hearth tax records those families who were able to pay as well as five people exempt as being too poor. (Appendix 2)

Toton remained a farming community, with the houses clustered near the Manor House. Local people worked on the land or for the Warren family. Benjamin Howard of Toton was a

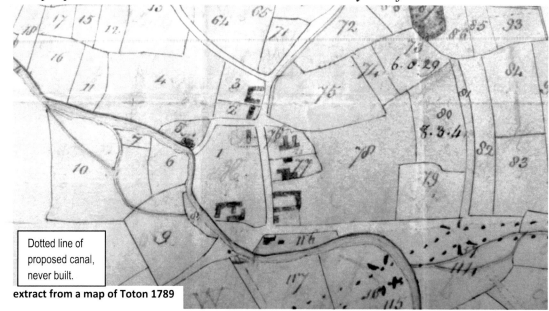

Dotted line of proposed canal, never built.

extract from a map of Toton 1789

footman to Lady Warren in 1833. He married Miss Harriet Allen[13], a housemaid to the same lady. Some people may also have worked in the Framework Knitting industry, using frames at home. Following the death of Sir John Borlase Warren and then Lady Caroline Warren, the heir to the estate was a child, William Vernon. It was during this time that the Railway made its appearance. Toton continued to be owned by the Warren family until 1855 when William Vernon sold the land to Richard Birkin, a lace manufacturer. His son Sir Thomas Isaac Birkin continued the tradition of centuries: to own Toton whilst living elsewhere, in his case Ruddington Grange. The Birkin family, including Mr Thomas Stanley Birkin, were involved with land in Toton and appear on the deeds of many properties in the area when the land was finally sold around 1921. Property developers moved in.

The 20th century was a century of growth and change for Toton. The hamlet expanded, housing development began and larger enterprises such as Chambers Packaging, various nursery gardens and even a military establishment were created. It was this growth and the demise of agriculture in the area that changed Toton forever.

---

[13] Derby Mercury November 1833

Travel around Toton – Long Eaton to Toton Corner

Toton South Junction and level crossing was, in the 1930s, an indication that one was approaching Toton. It was here in Long Eaton, (close to where Asda is now) that the railway crossed the A453 on its way to Toton Sidings. Life was slower at the beginning of the 20th century and not so busy.

Travelling eastwards towards Nottingham, the next Toton feature is St Leonard's Riding School. This too, is now in Long Eaton, although it began its life on High Road Toton. It sits beside the River Erewash.

Toton South Junction and level crossing 1933

The River Erewash

The River Erewash forms the boundary between the two counties, Derbyshire and Nottinghamshire for much of its journey. Although as it enters Toton, it begins to form this boundary, soon it meanders through Toton, flowing entirely through the Manor to join the River Trent. The name Erewash means 'wandering river' and wander it does, especially as it flows across the River Trent floodplain. Records show that owning the water rights was just as important, as owning the land. *"Half the River Erewash where it forms the Township boundary and the whole of the river where it runs through the Township. Half the River Trent is also included"*[1]. This is confirmed in the 1912 Kelly's Directory, where the acreage of the Toton Manor includes the acreage of water:- 1,331 acres and 57 acres of water. The River Erewash is not a navigable river, too shallow and with too many bends, necessitating the building of the Erewash Canal to transport goods, particularly coal.

The river itself has changed its course and has been altered on many occasions; in fact, on so many occasions that the original course of the river is not recognisable. Stretches of this river have been straightened and some of the banks strengthened with sand banks, perhaps in an effort to reduce the flooding that has frequently occurred. A mill race was constructed, at some time in the past and

River Erewash and road bridge

today two watercourses flow through Manor Park and under the A453 (now demoted to the A6005) from Long Eaton to Nottingham road, in a series of three bridges: Toton Arches.

---

[1] 1845 Rental Survey

"A new bridge was constructed over the Erewash in 1830. In 1911 the Road Board made a grant of £533 for the widening and improving of the series of bridges here not only for the benefit of traffic but also for the relief of floods.[1]

These two watercourses, River Erewash and By Pass channel (also known as Little Erewash) flow under different arched bridges and join together just south of the road. A straight separate stretch flows due south, from this point, avoiding many meanders and rejoins the main flow just before Attenborough junction (railway crossing with Barton Lane) The creation of the gravel pits in the

By Pass channel or Little Erewash

late 20th century encompassed the river. The latest channel to be dug, is one in the 21st century. This channel takes the Erewash out of the gravel pits, through which it has flowed for many years. It is hoped that the new channel will reduce pollution in the lake, as it diverts water from the Attenborough Nature Reserve (SSI[2]) and into the River Trent.[3]

The Rivers Erewash and Trent were very valuable assets, not only for fishing, but for osiers. These reeds would have been useful for thatching and fencing, as well as for basket making. Areas of osiers alongside the Erewash were rented out in the 19th century[4]. Two year old willows (osiers) were cut and auctioned in March. Crops were sold for £8 an acre in the 1800s, which multiplied by modern equivalents, shows this was a lucrative and necessary crop. Remnants of these trees still grow in Manor Park.

Willow bed beside the River Erewash

Fish was an important source of food, an income and for small boys a lot of fun. In the early 20th century Ernest Hall remembers *"In early September along the Canal bank, getting wasps nests for the grubs to take to Mears (over Derby Road bridge) who sold them to fishermen. I can't remember how much we got for them but I can say we got more wasp stings than pennies for the combs. Fishing for eels was a favourite pastime; apart from your own lines you could haul in other fishermen's lines, take the eels off – if any caught – and throw them in the basket. Camping on the osier beds by the River Erewash, making bows and arrows from the willows, fires and frying pans to eat these delicious eels"* The Erewash has been considered by many as "a capital fishing stream."[5]

---

[1] Then and Now R Mellors
[2] SSI =Site of Special Scientific Interest
[3] Cemex press release December 2nd 2009
[4] Derby Mercury advertisements 1878,1880, 1881 and 1882
[5] Derby Mercury September 1865

An article in a local newspaper in1986 records *"An excellent fishery in its lower reaches, especially when it flows through Attenborough gravel pit, just before joining the Trent."* The article considers the effect of the heavy industry further north and the consequences of effluence dumped in the river. Efforts were made in the 20th century to clean up the river. Today it is mainly coarse fish that swim in the waters. Chubb and the occasional pike or perch can be found in the shallow water of the wandering river.

The River Erewash, flows into the River Trent, another river once highly regarded for fishing. Salmon was caught for many years in the River Trent. The 1802 survey of Toton Manor records; *"In the fishery there are good salmon caught but not much small fish"* Over a hundred years earlier during the reign of King Charles I in the 17th century, there are records of numerous fish species: barbell, bream shad, grayling, lamprey, bullheads, stuttlebugs and many others. It was reported that sturgeon, salmon and smelts are accidentally entered into the Trent from the sea, whilst *"carp, trout and tenches are drove down by floods out of ye smaller brooks and ponds into the Trent. Sturgeon occurs yearly, salmon occur weekly in spring and summer."*[6]

Crossing the Erewash, the traveller finally arrives in Toton, Nottinghamshire.

Manor Garage alias Burnett's Garage

As the road bends, on it's journey towards Nottingham, a disused garage is now seen. In happier times it was known as Manor Garage or Burnett's Garage. It began life as a simple garage with a couple of petrol pumps, owned in the 1930s, by Mr John H Peake[7]. *"Mr Peake put two petrol pumps in the driveway (of Grange Farm) but then moved them to Toton Corner where the garage is now. There was no electricity in Toton and I remember taking an accumulator to Peat's garage to be charged."* (Mr Litchfield). *"How he (Peake) survived is a mystery. He sold petrol but to my knowledge only Fred Litchfield had a car."* (W. Whyatt) (memories of 1930s). The first petrol pumps were operated by hand, literally pumping the petrol from the tanks, with a sideways swinging motion, into the globe at the top of the pump where it then drained by gravity into the car.[8]

The garage, occupied the site of Mill Farm, whose farmhouse is seen in the picture below end on to the road.

Mr and Mrs Burnett and family bought the business from Mr Bob Smith and built a house behind the garage in the 1950s. Stan Burnett developed various small

Garage, filling the site of Mill farm

---

[6]Thoroton Vol 1898 page 30
[7] Kelly's Directory 1932
[8] Norman Lewis

businesses over a period of time. The central building housed a car sales section, before changing to accommodate second hand office furniture. During the 1960s, cars such as the Hillman Super Minx could be bought for £856 19 shillings, one of which, coloured Glen green and Foam white, boasted front disc brakes and improved seating[10]. Petrol sales continued for a while, along with bags of coal, until this became uneconomic.

Burnett's garage viewed from Long Eaton

A crane hire section was developed, with the huge cranes stored in a compound, beside the buildings. These could be seen for quite a distance. The crane hire section, begun with a French crane, was a successful venture. At one time there were fifteen large monsters for

Burnett's Garage end of 20th C

hire. Mrs Burnett remembers large cranes; one a 30 tonner, 'Hydracant,' was collected and driven down from Scotland. One huge 80 ton crane even came from Switzerland to join the fleet. These were a familiar sight to many people in the 1970s and 80s.

Mr Burnett, an engineer, who learnt his trade when apprenticed to Rolls Royce, enjoyed fast motor sports. Beginning

Crane hire section - Burnett's garage

---

[10] Long Eaton Advertiser Nov 1962

with motor bikes, he went on to enjoy motor car racing, visiting Silverstone on occasions. Later on in life, he obtained a pilot's licence and kept a small five-seater plane at Tollerton.

In 1954 the Burnetts built a large house, with a verandah overlooking the Erewash, behind the garage and enjoyed lovely views over the Trent floodplain. Even with such a close proximity to the

Stan Burnett racing at Silverstone

rivers, the house was never flooded. They acquired more land, after purchasing the adjacent shack and land once lived in by Oliver Marlow. It was a quiet and peaceful situation. Burnett's garage replaced a much earlier collection of buildings, known as Mill Farm.

House built circa 1954 behind Burnett's Garage

Mill Farm

Mill Farm existed until the mid 20th century, when it was demolished. It was rented from the Warren family and then later the Birkin family. Joseph Carter grew corn and milled it at the watermill close to the old Manor House,

Mill farm with William Roberts

before transporting the flour up the Trent, as far as Newark and Gainsborough. The farmland included some 'old turf' which is, perhaps, rough pasture, not suitable for arable crops as it would be subject to flooding. The farm had several scattered plots: close to the River Erewash, beside the Manor House and below the main road near the farm buildings.

Towards the end of the 19th century, the farm was listed in an auction sale (which included the sitting tenants) with over one acre as water and willows, whilst much of the rest is listed as "First Park, Second Park and Malt Rooms Moor". The two areas called Park were adjacent to the Manor House and watermill. The more prosperous land connected to Mill Farm was farmed by John Herrick who became a prominent member of the community, being part of the first Parish Council in 1894.[1]

The Carter family, is one of only a few families that have been linked to Toton for hundreds of years. The first known Carter was a Benjamin Carter, who was baptised in Attenborough church in 1761. He also lived and worked in Toton. Joseph, born 10th June 1797 at Mill Farm, married Mary Gusing, from Barton in Fabis and settled back in Toton where he died in 1879. All their six children were born

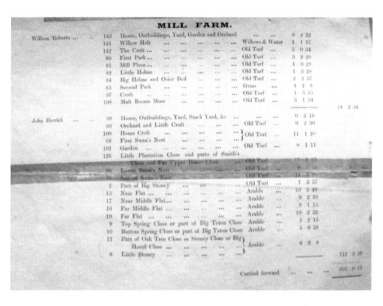

here. The fortunes of Joseph seem to have dwindled towards the end of the 19th century, as the census records the acreage he farmed reducing in size. By 1861, he is reduced to being a cottager and, although listed as a farmer in 1871, he only had around eighteen acres.[2]

William and Mary Roberts

Their youngest daughter, Mary, married William Roberts and they continued the tradition of farming until his retirement. Mary Carter attended school first in Toton, then in Long Eaton and finally in Nottingham. This couple were staunch Methodists and deeply connected to the Mount Tabor Church in Long Eaton. Mary appears to have been quite a character as she is noted as the second Florence Nightingale. *"....during the great scourge of 1862, when fever racked the homes of Long Eaton (and Toton) Mrs Roberts gave time and energy in nursing the fevered patients in their homes.[3]"* Mary lived to a ripe old age, and died, aged 94, in 1932.

Around the turn of the century, William and Mary Roberts moved out of Toton, to live in Long Eaton, where William died in 1916. Their children emigrated to various parts of the world.

---

[1] Parish meeting book PAC80/1/1
[2] Census 1861 and 1871
[3] Mary Carter's scrapbook

Mill Farm was situated on low lying land, a river floodplain and some of the land is now part of St Leonards Riding School. Horses graze where once cows chewed the cud. It was to this field that the dairy herd from Whyatts farm was brought morning and evening after milking. It was also on this field, in 1946, that horse racing took place. A small boy, who climbed a handy tree, thought that this was very exciting but the Council thought otherwise, being more concerned with traffic and the unlawful widening of a gateway to allow access. Concerns were raised about the potential of "hundreds of vehicles and thousands of people" visiting such an event.[4] Future events were banned.

Site plan of Mill Farm 1921 auction

The 1920s saw the beginning of a transformation. The land was sold and houses began to be erected on the higher land above the floodplain, alongside the road. The late 1940s or early 1950s saw buildings demolished and other facilities developed.

Notorious toilets Toton Corner

Toton Corner, the junction of High Road and Nottingham Road, was a prime spot for development. In the early 1950s a small brick building, housing some public toilets was built as another farm, Manor Farm came to the end of its life.

Also on High Road (the same side) an isolated house stands. This too was built in the early 1950s and was designed as a Police House, with an annexe for an office. It was occupied initially by P.C. Stirland and then by P.C. Frank Stopp, or "Copper Stopp" as he was known to some local boys. It was this officer who waited to catch the boys cycling across the Park and who completed his paperwork in the annexe office of the police house. P.C.Stopp worked from this house until 1958 when he

Former Police House

moved to Kirkby-in-Ashfield before returning to Toton when he retired around 1968. Toton is now policed from Beeston: the house has been converted and is now a family residence.

P.C.Stopp

Around 1900 Police Constables, were elected by the Parish Council. They stood for one year earning 10 shillings a year. Four nominations were always put forward, so maybe whoever was available took on the duty. Charles Bennett and John Smith were two of the nominees noted in the Parish Meeting Minutes in 1895.

---

[4] Beeston Gazette and Echo May and June 1946

Toton Corner

Manor Farm Recreation Ground formerly Manor Farm, alias Jeffery's Farm

The land between the River Erewash and Toton Corner was once part of Manor Farm. It was purchased by the Beeston and Stapleford District Council but, owing to local government reorganisation, is now owned by Broxtowe Borough Council and called Manor Farm Recreation Ground. It has become an area for leisure and recreation.

Manor House from Nottingham Road

The farm buildings were demolished in the 1950s, when the tenants left. The buildings became piles of rubble which were eventually cleared and landscaped. Several residents arriving in Toton around 1954 remember these piles of rubble. "*It was an eyesore.*" – Alf Barton. It appears the land was originally bought for a housing development, plans changed and a multi-purpose park evolved. Whilst in the throes of decision making and whilst there was no official playground nearby, some local children made the best possible use of the situation. "*Another favourite (place to play) though illegal, was Mr Jeffery's farm, with trees to climb and the mill pond to look for tadpoles and fish.*" (A Taylor.) "*I remember as a child, playing amongst the foundations, just a few courses of brick.*" (R.Wyatt). "*The mill pond was a good place for tadpoling.*" (K Harrison). The childrens' playground now sits beside this filled in depression and, as a young girl, Kathryn Harrison remembers rushing to be the first on the new metal slide when it was constructed.

The watermill, must have stood close to the old mill pond. The remnants of this important building can only be seen on old maps. Various millers rented out this building and once may have derived a good income from it. However, it sadly fell out of use in the 19th century, became a soap works and also a bone works before it finally collapsed. Odd, old stones remain in a nearby garden.

Old Gatepost beside footpath on High Road

Remnants too, of the Manor Farm complex are scant. One stone, the gatepost, and various humps and bumps are all that remain of this large collection of buildings in Manor Park.

The farm, known locally as Jeffery's Farm, was run by *"the autocratic Mr Jeffery, who considered himself something of a gentleman farmer."*[1] The farmhouse, a three-storey, red brick building, built in the mid 1700s, was surrounded by barns, a mill pond and orchards and sometimes flood water. A local man remembers the house as having no electricity; perhaps this was one of the reasons for its demise. The entrance to the house, off Nottingham Road, was that of a typical farmyard: muddy!

Manor House farm peeps over the hedges and floodwater

The Birkin family began to sell off parts of Toton Manor at the beginning of the 20th century. Mr Thomas Barton took the opportunity to diversify his business interests from the buses to farms. He bought Manor Farm and other parts of Toton and set up a dairy business. The farm was again tenanted, as it had been for centuries. Mr and Mrs Charles Jeffery and William Jeffery were the last tenants. Mrs Jeffery is remembered as

MANOR HOUSE FARM.

Tenants.	No. on Plan.	Description of Parcels.	Cultivation.	Particular Quantities. A. R. P.	Total Quantities. A. R. P.
		Brought forward ...	... ...		331 0 15
John Harby	91	House, Outbuildings, Yard, Stack Yard, Fold Yards, and Garden	... ...		
	90	Orchard	... ...	1 1 30	
	87	Willow Holt	... ...	0 3 5	
	88	Osier Holt and Garden	} Willows ...	0 3 7	
	93	Chapel Close	}		
	92	Paddock	} Old Turf ...	8 0 26	

sale of Toton Manor 1892 with sitting tenants

cycling to several houses with milk. A local resident remembers travelling from Chilwell during the War to collect eggs and milk to supplement their rations.

During the Second World War there were 'ack ack' guns stationed on the land. Searchlights were also fixed nearby at Coneries Farm, presumably to protect Chilwell Ordnance Depot and the railway.

The land farmed by the Manor tenants had shrunk, as centuries passed. Various folk maintained osier beds and parts of the Great Eastfield, which was one of the medieval fields

---

[1] Tony TAYLOR

bordering Chilwell. Other parts of the farm, in the 17th century, covered such fields as "The Ashes," "Swan's Nest" and the "Towne Meadow".

Toton Manor, an estate and Manor House, was also the administrative centre of Toton and Attenborough for years. A court was held in the Manor House, up to at least the beginning of the 17th century. Robert Mellors, writing at the beginning of the 20th century, records that there have been at least two large houses on the site. As the tallest house, in the area for centuries, at one time, the Manor House must have been an impressive sight. It is possible that there once was a chapel attached to the earliest Manor House. There is a reference to Chappell House, a parcel of the Demesne lands of the Manor or Lordship, in the marriage portion of John Jaques to Mary Edge (of Strelley Hall).[2] Maybe this house is either the old Manor House or a second farmhouse on the same site. However, by 1664 there is only one substantial house with John Jaques residing in it. The only other suggestion that there ever was a chapel is in the field names. John Jaques residing in the Manor House in 1664[3] paid rent for "the house, chapel close and orchard"[4] There was in the Lordship, "sufficient gorse in the parkes for brewing, baking and all such necessaries." It would have been a self sufficient unit.

> **Manor House** *The Manor House which four hundred and fifty years ago was the habitation of a lord was probably timber framed, the openings being filled in with stone, clay and other local material, for the making of bricks was then a lost art. The house was enclosed by a moat, traces of which may still be seen on the west, and north-western sides, near which the old water mill continued until less than a generation ago. A few stones are still to be seen as foundations of outbuildings, but the present brick house, now occupied by Mr Bates, can scarcely be two hundred years old. There is an old yew tree, and there are two yews in Mrs Benett's garden and her house appears to be the older one.*
> Then & Now R Mellors

Chapel Close was still named as a field name in 1892, as it was in 1847 when it was farmed by George Wragge, the High Constable of Broxtow Hundred.

The Manor House must have been a grand place once. It was the biggest house, with stables and barns. There would have been silverware, coaches and horses. The will of Arthur Warren

Manor Recreation Park 2000 from Nottingham Road, looking to the site of the Manor House

Senior, written in the Rent book, states he had two great silver candlesticks. He left these to his grandson while he bequested his silver porringer and spoon to Abigail Warren[5]. His son, in his will in 1694, gives his four best coach-mares to his dearest wife.[6]

---

[2] Marriage settlement John Jaques to Mary Edge DD/E 15/1 Nottinghamshire Archives
[3] Hearth tax
[4] Rent book DD 39/6 Details of holding in 1669 Mr John Jaques
[5] A rental of Toton DD/39/6 Nottinghamshire Archives

The site is now landscaped with tennis courts, a bowling green, a cricket square, a kickabout basketball area, a childrens' play area, a local nature reserve and space for activities such as football. Access is gained from several entrances, one of which has a handy little car park, off the High Road. There is a pleasant grassy area beside the River Erewash, on whose waters, the annual Duck Race takes place. January 2012 marked the 21st Duck Race when 1200 yellow plastic ducks were released into the River Erewash.[7] This winter activity of sponsoring rubber ducks, is a community family fun event, with money raised going to various charities. The ducks float down the river for about 600 yards to the bridge, with the owners of the first ten ducks receiving a prize. This fund raising event was enjoyed by over 600 people who sampled the mince pies and mulled wine, a feature of the winter season.

Penny Farthing Millenium sculpture

A sculpture created by a local man, commemorates both the Millenium and the National Cycle Route. Cycling, as a healthy and enjoyable sport, has seen a resurgence of the popularity, in the 21st century. An active Bowls club, enjoys a sunny site close to the High Road, with attractive spring flowering trees and colourful flower beds close by. The dog walkers and their dogs appreciate the freeedom of the area a far cry from the rubble and weeds of the 1950s.

Across the road, is another building taking its name from Toton Manor. The Manor, the pub on Toton Corner, has endured many changes over the years.

The Manor Pub (hotel) alias Kosie Cafe formerly Rosie's cafe

Toton Corner, the junction between High Road and Nottingham Road, is now festooned with traffic lights controlling the traffic from Long Eaton to both Nottingham and Stapleford. The most prominent feature is The Manor Pub. It has grown and expanded over the years, and in its time it has been a restaurant, a bed and breakfast business, a hotel, a cafe and was originally two private houses. A fish and chip shop stood at the rear of the building accessed by steps.

Manor Hotel, windows overlooking High Road circa 1980

The modern pub has developed from two old cottages that were labourers cottages at the beginning of the 20th century, occupied by Matthew Watts, a cowman, and John Musgrove, a waggoner[8] with his family. Ten years later another waggoner and his family had moved in. Residing in the other house, which had two small living

---

[6] Vernon Collection DVE 4/11 Chester Archives
[7] Beeston Express Jan 6th 2012
[8] 1901 census

rooms downstairs and three bedrooms upstairs, was Charles Pick, a horseman, with his wife, children and sister in law.[9]

This modern pub is reputedly haunted by a young woman. One can sit in the pub alcove imagining a young servant girl, maybe Martha, maybe Rose, ladling out rabbit stew after a long day in Manor Farm kitchens, before wandering round tidying up before going to bed.

Two houses became one house and then a cafe, Rosie's Cafe, where Parish meetings were sometimes held. In 1929 Parish meetings transferred from the old school to this building and councillors discussed weighty matters such as the erection of a new Council school, to serve the children of the village.

Mr & Mrs R.Skinner bought the property and changed the name of the cafe, to Kosie Cafe, prior to the Second World War. It became the public library for a time but *"in view of the unsatisfactory position regarding the return of books, the library centre at the Toton Café is to be closed immediately. The Notts Education committee has decided to re-open in the school as soon as possible."*[10]-

Mr & Mrs Skinner and Kosie Cafe staff circa 1940 and the dog

Kosie Cafe circa 1950

Mr Skinner arrived from London and opened the Kosy or Kosie Cafe coinciding with the opening of the Donnington Race Track – a half way stop from Nottingham. My first recollections are dozens of boy racers with bikes doped up with camphorated oil, stinking the place out. (W. Whyatt)

Mr Taylor bought Cosy Cafe, following the move by the Skinner family to Grange Farm. Mr Arthur Taylor, was the organist at the Albert Hall, in Nottingham and used to give music lessons. *"I don't think we ever used the Cosy*

The Manor - became part of the- a Tom Cobleigh pub chain, for a short time

[10] Beeston Gazette 1940

Café, except to buy the occasional ice-cream, but I did go there every week (1950s) from the age of about seven, for my music lessons with Mr Taylor." (H. Knewstubb)

The Caress family followed and developed the business into a thriving hotel with nineteen rooms, a residents' lounge and dining room. Mr & Mrs Alan Caress sold it again some thirty-two years later, for £300,000. Tom Cobleigh took over the hotel, using the adjacent pair of semi-detached houses as the hotel annexe before demolishing them to extend the car park. It is now a pub cum diner, a family friendly business.

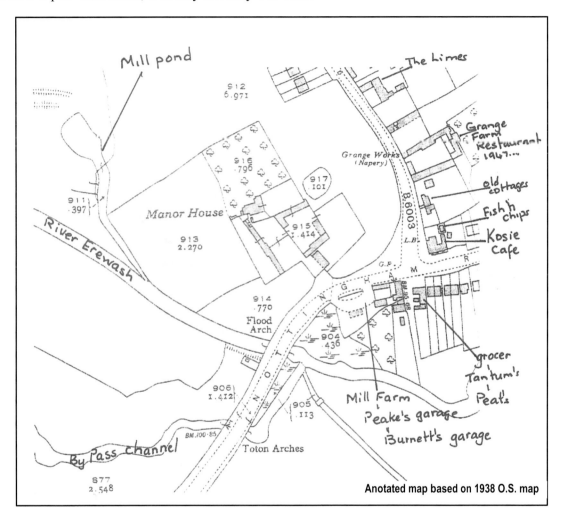

Anotated map based on 1938 O.S. map

On the opposite side of Nottingham road, were several small shops. These shops included a cobbler's and a hut housing the village newsagent. (E. Knewstubb)

Bernard Marshall, a real Toton character, began his business here (with a little bookmaking on the side) before moving to a piece of waste land on Portland road. A row of semi detached houses were built. Number 355 (near the garage) became a grocer's; Tantums then Stathams (1930s, 1940s,) and finally Oswald Peat (1950s) ran businesses here. Toton Corner, today, is a relatively peaceful place, with just the traffic rumble, a sign of twentieth century progress. *In the 1950s, it was the roar of the motor bikes as they revved up having stopped off at the cafe for a cuppa.* (W. Whyatt)

Improvements have taken place, with various road widening schemes and planting programmes, designed to enhance the safety and appearance of this corner. Bulbs enhance the verges in Spring, whilst summer colour shines from the tiered planter on the corner.

Between the shops and Mill Farm there was a track leading to a cycle repair hut at the rear of the farm owned by Oliver Marlowe, one of Toton's "characters". (R Wyatt)

"At Toton Corner there was a shop and a massage parlour (now a hairdressers). Then various odd job people had businesses in buildings now demolished (once barns from Mill Farm?) and now Burnett's garage." (E. Hall)

The hairdresser was Miss Acton, who was also a trained masseuse. There was a barber there as well. The Sunday School met above Miss Acton's, for a short time, in the 1940s. This room was converted into a flat, in the next decade.

Toton had few shops. *We didn't have a butcher in Toton, as far as I can remember, so Mum got our meat from Mr Barker, in Long Eaton. He*

Shops and houses south side of Nottm Rd 2012

would deliver about twice a week (no fridges or freezers then). There was no 'shopping around.' We stayed loyal to the same shop. We always had to get shoes from Mr Horobin, at Hilton's – even if I preferred the ones in Trueform! Other purchases usually had to come from the Co-op, so that we got the divi(dividend). Most of our clothes were home-made, often make do and mend, or hand- me-downs. I can still remember my little brother announcing to a long bus queue, "These are my new trousers. Mummy made them out of an old pair of Uncle Ken's. Mum used a razor blade to cut the toes out of my leather sandals, so I could wear them a bit longer". When I was old enough to go to Long Eaton on my own, I loved going into Woolworths. (H. Knewstubb)

Mr and Mrs Reginald Skinner, are reputed to have also owned property on Nottingham Road and billeted officers in the Second World War; however it is a G Skinner who is listed in 341 – 343 Nottingham Road. *"Mr Skinner was made with World War ll. It got better, the troops in Chilwell were in nice cosy Nissen huts but the officers living out were catered for by Mrs Skinner. He (Reg Skinner) first purchased empty houses[11] opposite (Kosie Cafe) to accommodate officers and their wives which must have been successful as he quickly acquired Grange farm and transformed that into an exclusive officers' mess."* (W. Whyatt)

A good bus service links Toton with Nottingham and Long Eaton, travelling every few minutes along Nottingham road, but many villagers bewail the loss of the Barton bus service, which used to run from Ilkeston to Shardlow via Toton and the High Road.

---

[11] Nos 341-3 Nottingham Rd – Street Directory

High Road -The Old Cottages of Toton

The area around Toton Corner to the junction of Stapleford Lane and Chetwynd Road, is the nucleus of the old Township of Toton. Now called the High Road, this was once the main Turnpike road to Nottingham. There are still several old cottages which date back several hundred years.

The first of these, Cottage Cattery, is thought to be an eighteenth century dwelling. The building appears on the 1847 and 1789 maps and may either be older or have replaced an earlier building. The house, now one, was originally two cottages occupied by farm workers

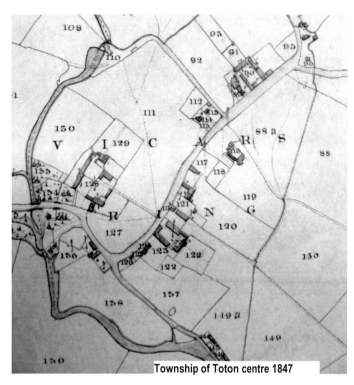

Township of Toton centre 1847

like Benjamin Clarke, milkseller, his wife Catherine and their daughters. They had just three small rooms, one of which was the kitchen.[1] It still retains the old character of the 18th and earlier centuries, being a long cottage, one room width, with room connecting to room.

It was modernised in the 1940s by Mr Veale, with the addition of a bathroom and kitchen built on to the length and rear of the building. The beams still support the low ceiling. At some time, electricity was added. To the rear, the garden once a large prosperous orchard would have been part of a much larger plot.

The early 17th century houses would have developed from the medieval buildings with a long room and maybe a shelter at one end for the animals. A single storey thatched cottage with a central hearth was a feature of this period.

Old High Road Cottage- now a cattery

Catherine Clarke and daughters, High Rd cottage –-1913

---

[1] 1911 census

This building still had its thatched roof until the 1930s or 40s.

The Hearth tax of 1664 and 1674[2] records the number of buildings – 11 and their inhabitants (see Appendix) but some of these, would have been near the church, in Attenborough. In 1674, the records show an increase in prosperity, as in that year several of the properties have two hearths and Arthur Warren (replacing John Jaques in the Manor House) had seven. It was during the 17th century that bricks became more widely available. A law introduced in 1671 stated that

Toton	1664	charge
Occupier	Hearths	tax
John Jacques	5	10s
Thomas Coming	1	2s
John Black	1	2s
George B ?ker	1	2s
John Canner	1	2s
George Johnson	1	2s

bricks had to be a standard size: 9 inches by 4½ inches and 2 ¼ inches deep. Bricks were then added to a timber-framed building by encasing it or just filling in the gaps.

Two more old cottages remain. Both are on the High Road, near Portland Road junction. The first, a pair of cottages which have been converted into one house, has an interesting collection of finds, giving some idea of its past. A child's leather shoe with a blunt toe was found behind a chimney. The shoe dates from the second half of the nineteenth century, circa 1860. Such shoes were put in place when alterations or buildings works occurred, to ward off witches. Only a single shoe, often a child's worn-out shoe, was hidden so that a malevolent spirit could not steal it and take away the protection that a shoe gives. The little shoe, a

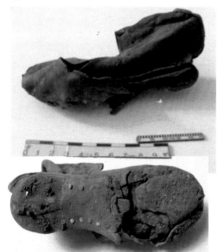

remnant of a laced boot, was definitely worn, the sole is nearly through but the little hob nails remain.

Other finds include a Second World War helmet, lots of bottles, with their thick glass and varied inscriptions, and broken clay pipes. Tobacco was an expensive commodity during the 17th century, necessitating a small bulbous bowl, with little or no decoration. Various decorated and plain pipes have been discovered. Fluted designs were introduced by a family of pipe makers called Turpin, who were making these clay pipes between 1770 and 1835 in Newark, a place which Joseph Carter, from Mill Farm,

travelled to by boat with his cargo. It is therefore possible that Newark was the origin of these pipe fragments, used by working men in Toton.

Clay pipe with fluted decoration

The cottage, with its narrow 2½ inch bricks, has many levels of floor. The oldest part of the house, would have been the narrow single room width. Additions such as back two back pantries, showed an increase in prosperity. The ceilings still contain the reeds, with lime mortar. Items, such as, reeds would have been available locally.

Plain clay pipe remnant

---

[2] Thoroton

The well, now firmly capped, remains in the garden. It would have produced good clear water, as it ran over the glacial gravels. A well was an important necessity before 20th century plumbing systems.

Deeds of the cottages, like many others in Toton, only go as far back as 1921 when the estate

The cottages at Toton.

PROTEST AT DEMOLITION OF COTTAGES

began to be sold off. They reveal past owners including Robert Oliver Marlowe who, like his predecessors, rented out the cottages. He bought the two cottages for £250, taking out a mortgage for £150 from a basket maker in Castle Donnington. Former cottage names also occur, referring to 71 High Road as Rose Cottage in 1936.

These cottages, once threatened with demolition in 1978, survived after Toton residents protested. The Chairman of the Residents Association collected a petition and stated that the pair of cottages, with an acre of land, was said to be over 250 years old. There was a fight to save the cottage and luckily for Toton, saved it was. Indeed the cottages are marked on a map dated 1789 and maybe are earlier still.

Next door to this cottage, is Sunnydene, another old cottage and also on the old maps. Remnants of Tudor brickwork are still evident in the internal chimney breast. Another feature of an earlier time is the metal hook, in the chimney on which a pot would have hung to boil the stews or other meals.

Rumour has it that a ghost was in residence and that it moved items such as the poker on the fireplace. This ghost has not been seen or heard of for many years. Perhaps it is happy with its present family and prospect of a pleasant future.

Sunnydene 2012

All the old cottages have changed over the centuries, with repairs to crumbling brickwork, additions and extensions to fit in with modern living.

The cottages, are thought to have been the homes of agricultural labourers. Situated between Whyatts Farm and Manor Farm, work such as hay making, animal husbandry and ploughing, along with other manual jobs, would have been available. Remnants of a few of the old farmhouses can still be seen, but most have disappeared.

Hike up High Road – Turnpike Road

The High Road has other interesting buildings, some of which, like The Limes remain, whilst other buildings with long histories have disappeared. Grange Farm is one of the latter.

Grange Farm

Grange Farm, for many years known as the best restaurant in the area (during the middle part of the 20th century) possibly began life in 1691 during the reign of William and Mary and was bought in the early 1940s by the Skinner family.

Grange Farm Restaurant, carvery and banqueting suite

The date 1691, carved in the main beam of the entrance hall, was for many years covered with plaster. It was rediscovered when the plaster was removed during renovation work after a change of ownership in 1944.

Grange Farm must have had a chequered history. It does not feature in the written documents as a farm, although it clearly grew into one over the years. It has been the home of various tenant farmers and their families for centuries. John Brex Smith was the tenant farmer in 1892. He farmed 135 acres at that time. It was a mixed farm with some arable land and pasture. His stepson, Benjamin Clarke, was a dairyman here in the early 20th century.

Pigs were another feature of the agricultural scene. Salt pork was an important feature in the larder of nineteenth century farmhouses. Young and breeding pigs were allowed to range free, while those for fattening were kept in pigsties.[1]

This farm was owned by the Birkin family and sold in 1921 in seven lots. It seems to have been used in smaller units, from this time on, with much of the

John and Mary Smith Grange farm   1909

land sold for housing. One of the lots was sold to Alfred. Woodforth, who built a large bungalow, with a long garden, fronting Nottingham Road. The auction, advertised the premises as suitable for business use. John James Holland became involved with the Trent Valley Sports & Social Club, which

---

[1] Norman Lewis- Land Use

utilised the barns. He later moved into the farm.[2] The barns began to be used for various purposes. A neighbour remembers her husband rented space in one, for his car.

After the First World War, it (Grange Farm) was used as a club and they had a bowling alley where Grange Farm restaurant was. The barn was used to card lace. Nearing the end of the Second World War Grange Farm became available for sale. Mr and Mrs Skinner, who owned the Cosy Café, had a Bed and Breakfast business. Because the B & B was very popular Mr and Mrs Skinner's two daughters had to give up their beds for guests, they decided to buy Grange Farm as a family home. Two of my cousins from Portugal who came over to join the RAF, one was just 21 and the other was coming up to 21 so my mother asked Mr Skinner if he could provide a party for them in the Cosy Cafe. He suggested that it could be held in Grange Farm. Among the guests were two couples who were going to be married soon. Mr Skinner said he would hold the reception in the granary and I went to help them white wash the walls. This is how Grange Farm (the restaurant business) *started.* (M Litchfield)

Mr and Mrs Reginald Skinner purchased the buildings around 1944. When they moved in, they not only rediscovered the date on the beam but also discovered some lace machines in the barn[3], left over perhaps when the barns were used as 'outworkings' for various lace businesses in nearby Long Eaton. Jobs such as finishing-off would be done by outworkers.

Life during the 1940s, must have been very difficult. Rationing continued. Ration cards were distributed from several places. Toton folk had to walk to Stapleford (Johnson and Barnes opposite Park Street) in 1946. A plea was made the next year to improve the arrangements. It was considered *"a disgrace for the women to push their prams all that way"*.[4] Arrangements were made to collect the new ration books at Grange Farm, the (Food / A.R.P.) Office to be open for three days in July.

During the War, meals were prepared for the ATS and army personnel. Mr and Mrs Skinner held a few birthday parties in the barn and from that grew the idea of a restaurant. Early visitors to Grange Farm parties remember the iron rings on the walls used for the cows, remnants of its former use as a cowshed. From small beginnings, the business grew.

Grange Farm restaurant with coffee lounge extension

Mr & Mrs Skinner sold Kosie Cafe and took some of the staff including Catherine Clarke, step daughter of John Smith, (farmer) to work in their new restaurant. Catherine Clarke continued to work there for the rest of her life, up to her death aged eighty. Another

[2] Electoral roll 1937
[3] Newspaper report on closure-Jan 20th 1995
[4] Beeston Gazette and Echo May 1947

prominent member of staff was Ivy Howitt, a tall girl who began working as a waitress and then became Head Waitress for many years.

The Restaurant opened for business in 1947 catering for small private parties and, after extensive alterations to the stables and milking parlour, it fully opened in 1949 as Grange Farm Restaurant. (menu Appendix 4)

The cowsheds and stables were converted into a restaurant and the old barn became the ballroom. Dinner dances were often held here.

PART OF RESTAURANT
These were originally Cowsheds and Stables

THE BALLROOM

It became a popular venue for a special occasion, such as a wedding or an anniversary. Extensions and improvements followed and many prestigious groups such as the Rotary Club took advantage of the facilities. Various civic functions were also held here.

Mrs and Mrs Nance Skinner were well known and active figures in Toton, with connections with several groups. Mrs Skinner started the Women's Social Service club. This group held an exhibition of handicraft and needlework in June 1949, in order to raise money to save Toton Manor House and buy it as a Community Centre. The 250 items were locally made by some of the two hundred members and "tastefully arranged in the main dining hall on the farm."[5] This Ladies' group also enjoyed visits to places of interest, such as Wedgewood Pottery in 1955. Mrs Nance Skinner, as a leading figure of the community, opened galas and fetes including the Conservative Association's Summer Fete on one occasion.

Women's Social Service club with Lady Belper centre, 1952

Mr Skinner was an eminent Rotarian, accounting for the vast number of occasions when the Rotary Club met at Grange Farm.

Grange Farm, was for many years the pre-eminent restaurant in the district, attracting customers from a wide area. The festive season was a very busy period, with around 13,000

[5] Nottingham Journal 27.6.1949

customers in a twenty-two day period.[6] Famous faces were also seen. Fanny Craddock, David Essex and Des O'Connor dined here, during nearly fifty years of the farm being a restaurant.[7] Richard Dimbleby also dined at Grange farm, when he chaired an "Any Questions" broadcast in the area[8]. Bookings were taken months, if not years in advance but all good things come to an end. The last Christmas meal was served on Christmas Eve, 1994.

Grange Farm with exit from car park onto High Road circa 1990

Grange Farm was auctioned off in January 1995, with all the fittings and furnishings included in the sale, even the whitebait and ice-cream from the freezer, were on the list and sold to the highest bidder. £370 was paid for an original British Telecom phone box, in the ballroom. Lots were even stuck to the Christmas trees and the decorations left hanging after the last festive meal.[9]

Today Grange Farm has gone, demolished, at the end of the 20th century, along with its large car park. The land was sold for building. Grange Close, a modern housing development, honours the memory of the past.

Close to Grange Farm, a cottage once stood on the High Road. Sanday Wallace, a wheelwright, worked in the workshops, behind this small one roomed building, where a tall, thin man used to sit outside. He was possibly Charlie Mann (Manley) "*A big chap who leant over the stable door, who shouted and terrified us children*". (N.Lewis) A hundred years earlier this small workshop was a farrier's, classed as a hovel or small open sided building.

The farrier, handy for the farms, is not mentioned again so one can suppose that William Eaton from the blacksmiths took his trade.

Near Grange Close, adjacent to Norfolk Avenue and High Road, another old building still stands.

Demolition of Grange Farm,

[6] Neighbourhood News 13.1.1999
[7] Neighbourhood News 13.1.1999
[8] S.Wilkinson
[9] Newspaper report 20.1.1995

The Limes

The Limes, takes its current name from the many Lime trees, in the area. There is speculation that these were planted at the same time as the Lime trees in Stapleford, by Sir John Borlase

The Limes 2012

Warren, when he made great improvements and changes to Stapleford Hall, as some of these trees, with their wide girth appear to be aged specimens. The Limes, is another of Toton's buildings with a history going back centuries.

It was once a farm or small holding, whose land extended to Chilwell, where the present Corn Mill Pub stands. Fields were rented as far as Barton Lane and at one time, the tenant farmer, Mr Charles

Bennett, rented land in the Banks Road area. The farm, like many others had a productive vegetable garden and orchard. The barn had holes in the wall for doves to enter their roosting places, which were internal wooden shelves attached to the wall, a kind of mini dovecote.[10] The far field was used for hay, then used by the War Department, and is now a modern housing estate, accessed from Norfolk Avenue. The Long Eaton Soldiers' and Sailors' Club used a field for football, as did Cranfleet Football Club. The Bennett family and the Litchfield family once lived in this old house. Mr W.Roe recalls stories told by his relations.

"Grandfather Bennett was a farmer in Tutbury before moving to Toton just before the First World War and occupied The Limes. When the Great War started and the Shell Filling factory was built all the arable land was taken from The Limes. The only income the farm had then was from the milk that was produced. For this milk delivered to Attenborough railway station they got 1½d (old pennies) per gallon, so three of Mr Bennett's daughters decided to sell milk to the munition workers coming from the factory (down Chetwynd Road). They sold this milk at sixpence per glass and soon made a lot of money. They made sufficient money to buy the Coneries Farm down

The Limes farmyard with doves

---

[10] Janet Davison

Barton Lane. I have been told by my cousin that, when the explosion at the Shell Filling Factory happened, she was sitting with her Grandad in the walled garden next to The Limes and that the garden was used as a Clearing Station.

The Limes Farm with original cow sheds built around the mid 1500s and farmhouse added later is aptly named from the numerous lime trees on the property. It is an imposing building conveniently situated on the Toton to Stapleford road near to its junction with the main Nottingham to Derby road some 300 yards away and forms three sides of a square with garden and lawn in the space between. To the south side a tall brick wall separates the house from a large vegetable garden which runs back well beyond the rear limits of the house proper. On the north side are the brick cow sheds. Between the boundaries, forming the third side of the square, are the living quarters of the house.

Stables of old farm became part of St Leonard Riding school

The two entrances to the farm, both enclosed by tall black painted galvanised iron sheets, were next along the road. The first led into the farm whilst the second led into spare land containing a barn and stables (later sold to St Leonards Riding School). Through the main gates on the right were the milking stalls for the 8-10 cows. All the buildings were co-joined and around the far corner of these sheds, a stone staircase led up into the roof space (hayloft) over the stalls, a favourite place for poultry. (Local history has it that this area was a Methodist chapel and that John Wesley the founder of Methodism preached here circa 1770.)

Rear of The Limes with stone staircase to hayloft

Next along this back wall a small door led into the cooler over which the milk was poured to cool before being poured into the churns. From here, a small inner door led straight into the dining room, the lounge and eventually into the kitchen. Outside there was a fair space for the cattle to roam before being driven to local pasture – of which there was ample space for all four farms in the immediate area – with a stone water trough up against the kitchen wall. There was a large orchard, suitably fenced, adjacent to this space with a side path, normally with a haystack or two, leading to fields where the near one was used for grazing and the distant one for hay in the summer and by Cranfleet F.C. in the winter. A separate path in this latter field led directly to the main road, thus not encroaching on the farm proper. (This field was bought by the War Department on the outbreak of World War II and incorporated into Chilwell Ordnance Depot.)

George and Nellie Dakin bought The Limes in the early 1920s. George had trained as a lace machine engineer but had been interned in Germany during the First World War. For health reasons he decided to buy a farm as this would be beneficial to his health. It became predominantly a dairy farm. Two milkings (by hand) a day with morning and afternoon deliveries around Toton and Long Eaton was normal procedure, with the morning one sometimes delayed when the pony was disinclined to be caught. Road traffic was light at this time with very few cars, delivery being mainly by horse and cart. Dakin's milk float was a two wheeled affair, loaded with two or three large churns and 1 pint and a ½ pint ladle for filling the customer's jug or basin. On the advent of bottled milk in the 1940s and an increasing demand for it, George had the ideal solution. His practice was to keep a crate of empty bottles on the float and fill them direct from the churn just before arriving at the customer's door. The bottles were then sealed (with thumb pressure) with a thick circular disc with a perforated middle. Not very hygienic but no-one complained.

Although small, the farm was obviously profitable and it wasn't long before George said goodbye to the pony and bought a little blue van (DNN 540) for his milk deliveries. Not only that, he had a Wolseley motor car, with illuminated logo on the bonnet and real leather upholster, in which he used to visit relatives who owned a farm in Kegworth.

The Limes farm is now owned (1998) and has been for many years by Alan Patchitt and sons, a high class joinery company. His wood and all the paraphernalia of that trade now occupies the stalls where Dakin's cows stood to be milked." (W. H Roe 1998)

Erewash Blinds now occupy the premises from where the joinery shop once traded from.

Stableyard and tack room of St Leonards Riding school.

St Leonards Riding School
St Leonards Riding School began its career, at The Limes. Bill Davison bought the farmyard in 1946 and erected an old Nissen hut behind the stables, where some ponies were stabled. He named the Riding School for his favourite place, Chapel St Leonards, where he and his wife Solai would ride to (with an over-night stop).

Two fields were rented for lessons; one from the Patchitts who were now in The Limes and one field from Moor House (Mr Litchfield). Grazing for the horses was beside Nottingham Road, where the current Riding School is. The original stabling and pasture for the horses was part of Limes Farm in the mid 20th century; the stables, probably being the homes for the working horses of the farm, before becoming home to many riding ponies. A cinder track was laid behind the stables where riding lessons were given. Miss Gladys Warren worked for Bill

Davison for many years. She was a patient and good teacher who died within days of the death of Bill in 1976. That year was a momentous one for the School, as it was following the purchase of all the fields by Westerman, the builder that St Leonards had to move to the Nottingham Road site. The High Road stables were demolished and new houses created; Evesham Court came into being.

Gymkhanas were held on Manor Recreation Park, where Lombardy Lodge is now, for many years before moving to a field adjacent to the present site of the Riding School, on Nottingham Road. Hattie Jaques, the television and film celebrity, even presented

Gable end of Patchitt's now Erewash Blinds looking at the new houses of Evesham Court

Hattie Jaques with a rosette for Sally Davison

Gymkhana 1954 Toton recreation Ground

the prizes on one occasion.

Two other substantial houses, The Knoll, and Moor House once fronted the High Road, but are now hidden behind more modern houses.

Moor House

Moor House, recently used as a dentists, was in former times a prosperous corn merchant's business. Mr Fred Litchfield, the corn merchant, was a prominent member of Toton's community, being a councillor and a sidesman at St Mary's, Attenborough. A large corrugated corn store which stood in the grounds parallel to the road was pulled down, when the area was redeveloped, circa 1972, after the demise of the business. The area had dramatically changed from an agrarian economy with associated agricultural products to a village requiring residential developments for nearby expanding industries in Chilwell and Nottingham.

Moor House

The demand for grain was no longer there and there were no longer farms supplying the grain. The land became used for housing and is now occupied by Kensington Close, thus reducing the resident rat population that had been enjoying the grain.

Moor House is an old house, dating back to before 1789, when it appears on a map. The Moor was part of Muckle Moor or Great Moor. The Muckle Moor and the Great Eastfield were two of the medieval fields managed with strip farming. The Moor, in this part of Toton, would have been tussocky grassland flooded by the brooks that crossed the land, on their way to the Trent.

Kensington Close -2012

It was an area of pasture or lowland rough grazing. It appears to have covered a considerable part of Toton. " *Land called the Moors is at present wet, its produce a scanty moderate herbage, but admits sufficient decent for drains to be made at small expense to lay the same thoroughly dry which measure would double the present value of the land. No 27 is a very sound good piece of land in high condition. The remainder of the land being called Muckle Moor is much addicted to flooding, is the inferior piece of land in the estate nor does there appear any probable method of improvement. The arable land is well managed"*.....Surveyors report 1788[11]

Hidden away behind more houses, is The Knoll, one of the early 20th century additions to Toton. It's grounds have shrunk whilst nearby housing developments have grown.

Another interesting building on the High Road is number 76. Although not as old as any of the houses mentioned so far, the house has developed from two railway carriages. *Until 1951, the local milkman was Mr Elliot, who lived at no. 76 High Road in a bungalow he had built, based around two railway carriages. When he retired, the business and the premises were purchased by Mr Les Ebbern, who traded for about eleven years before selling the round to the Co-op. I worked for Mr Ebbern at weekends from 1952 until leaving school in 1956 and for the first year we were still delivering milk to houses by ladling it out from a bucket (a specially-made container with a lid) into the customers' jugs – not very hygienic by today's standards!" (A.Taylor)*

Number 76 was the last 'even' house on the High Road on one's journey to Beeston. Here the road turned east. On the 'Odd side' on the corner of Portland Road, is a newsagent's formerly run by Bernard 'Barney' Marshall.

Portland Road corner to St Peter's, High Road

Further up High Road, where St Peter's Church now stands, stood the old village school.

---

[11] DD/WN/54 Survey and rental of the Manor of Toton 1788 – Nottinghamshire Archives

Toton Endowed School alias Village School

The old village school was endowed by Lady Caroline Warren, of Stapleford Hall. It is a notable fact that Toton Endowed School began prior to the school in Stapleford which was also set up by Lady Warren. This school began life in the 1830s. It was especially aimed at the poor children of the parish. The first teacher was Robert Shaw, who was soon replaced by two teachers; Daniel Roper and his wife Mary. Their daughter Eliza (who married John Herrick) joined the team and continued teaching from the mid 1800s until 1922. The school was to accommodate two teachers and sixty children aged from 5 to 11. Rules laid down by Lady Warren stipulated that corporal punishment was not allowed and that clothing would be provided for the poor children of Toton. Clothing, an early uniform, was provided initially.

TOTON.

SCHOOL BALANCE SHEET FOR YEAR ENDING NOV. 30, 1911.

RECEIPTS.	£	s.	d.	EXPENDITURE.	£	s.	d.
Balance in hand	3	9	8	Salaries	56	1	0
Dividends	49	14	0	Fuel	6	0	6
School pence	2	7	1	Books and stationery	1	5	3
Birkin, Sir Thomas	5	0	0	Riddle	0	1	4
Hughes, Rev. A. E.	1	0	0	Repairs to building	1	1	6
Smith, Mrs. F. C.	10	0	0	Repairs to paths	0	10	0
				Painting, etc.	1	12	10
				Cleaning School, chimney and ashpits	2	12	0
				Cleaning materials	0	8	0
				Prizes	0	7	1
				Insurance	0	9	0
				Tithe	0	0	10
				Balance in hand	1	1	5
	£71	10	9		£71	10	9

The Week-night Services have been hearty and well-attended. It is encouraging also to notice an increase in the Sunday School.

Every Sunday.—2.30 p.m., Sunday School.
Every Wednesday.—2.30 p.m., Sewing Meeting ; 7 p.m., Service in School.

extract from parish magazine

The school had a good reputation. A report in 1912 records; "The work done in this school is very good and quite equal to what one ought to expect in so small a school." The same year, though, an unfortunate incident occurred: a fire. *"We are full of thankfulness for the preservation of our school buildings. Through an accident caused by a little dog, the school house caught fire. Happily the fire was soon discovered and Mrs Herrick with the help of a kind passer by, extinguished the flames before much damage was done to the building. Furniture and clothes suffered more but things might have been worse. We praise God."* [12]

The church magazine for Attenborough parish has a few mentions of this little school. Another weekly event, for some years, was the sewing circle, led by Mrs Birkin.

Towards the end of the school's life, two local ladies, Mrs Litchfield and finally Miss Catherine Day, taught just thirty children, under nine years

Mrs Litchfield at Toton Endowed school 1924

---

[12] Attenborough Parish magazine

of age.

Mrs Litchfield, wife of Fred Litchfield and sister of William Bennett, taught here for a while, before becoming a Manager at the new school – Toton County School. Mrs Edith Litchfield and her husband began to breed pedigree fowls. *"My mother used to come back home at lunchtime to check which fowl had laid an egg as they were all trap nested. My father got the idea of producing eggs in winter and kept some white fowls in one of our outbuildings and fed them on a mixture of grain and protein. He got these fowls to lay in winter which was very unusual and very lucrative so then he started to market the mixture as an Egg a Day mash. He then formed the firm F.W.Litchfield and Co Ltd."* (M. Litchfield)

Internal view of Toton Endowed School

Miss Catherine Day, came to teach at this school in the mid 1920s, following Mrs Edith Litchfield. She is remembered with affection and respect. She was the only teacher and therefore taught the whole curriculum with particular emphasis on good manners, cleanliness, religion and the 3 R's: Reading Writing and 'Rithmetic.

Round the walls blackboards were fixed so that we could draw on them – mostly biblical pictures where the Lord was always depicted by a cross. We used slates and chalk to learn our alphabet on. As it was a church school we all had to take our own hymn books and sang hymns every day with Grace at the start and finish of every session. The Vicar from Attenborough came quite often to teach us and to test our knowledge of the bible. (E. Hall)

TOTON SUNDAY SCHOOL NOTES
The Sunday School Harvest Thanksgiving was held in the Day School, Chetwynd Road, on October 14. The school room was piled up with flowers and fruit and vegetables, the abundance suggesting the bounty of God's gifts. There were about 70 children, and fifty adults present when the Vicar began the service. Miss D. Tatman, the superintendent, with her assistant teachers, had arranged an interesting panorama for the children. The well-known hymns were thoroughly enjoyed, and the children did their parts with keenness and pleasure. It was a happy service.
From Parish magazine- Attenborough Church

The Sunday School also met here and transferred to the Council School on Chetwynd Road in 1933. The afternoon class began at 2.30 on a Sunday afternoon. In 1922 Mrs Litchfield was the teacher. In later years Miss Tatman, Miss Cooke, Mr Riley and Miss Stimpson among others played their part. Miss Dorothy Tatman was for many years the superintendent of the Sunday School. She was not a professional teacher but ran the school very efficiently and was respected by the children. Mr Loxton followed her when she left the area in 1950.

Events such as Harvest Festivals and Prize Giving occurred annually. *"Toton Sunday School Harvest Festival was attended by 60 children and 24 adults on 27th October 1940. It raised 16 shillings which was sent to East London, Vicar of Bermondsey, St Luke's vicarage."*

Toton Sunday School: *The Prize Giving was held on December 29th 1947, when the Vicar of Attenborough presented books to 70 children for good attendance.*" (Parish Magazine)

Toton Endowed School closed in 1933, as it was in a bad state of repair. The building was then used by Rice and Beck, Builders and Joiners, while its fate was being decided. It was eventually demolished, shortly after World War ll. Under the terms of the endowment the land had to be used for the education of local children and to be kept within Anglican bounds. It was therefore decided to build a Hall Church to be used by the Sunday School, where local Church services could also be held.

Builders and Contractors

B. RICE & D. BECK
LIMITED

HIGH ROAD · TOTON · BEESTON

St Peter's Church

St Peter's Church 1954

Fund raising began after the War and this supplemented the money accrued from the winding up of the Endowment Trust set up by Lady Caroline Warren. The Trust was wound up in summer 1952 by the Southwell diocese and work began on planning a venue for the Sunday school and a village hall to serve the community.

The initial plans were scaled down, because of the cost and in 1954 St Peter's Hall Church opened. Large blue folding doors closed off the sanctuary when not in use and the sanctuary itself had three square windows high in the wall. These were replaced several years later. The Hall Church of St Peter gradually prospered and developed until it eventually became St Peter's Church. Since then it has extended its size, its range of activities and now is a well established church with a thriving congregation. It became a separate independent parish, ratified by her Majesty in 2001, bucking the trend for parishes to amalgamate.

In the early years, donations were received with gratitude for the many pieces of furniture that were needed. A clock was donated by Douglas Hall: an electric clock that ticked loudly, a clock that collected many comments over the years. A harmonium was donated which sufficed until a piano and, finally, a pipe organ was obtained. Nowadays a modern keyboard is available for services.

TOTON NOTES

A Sale of Work followed by a social evening was held on Saturday, November 3, in aid of the Sunday School Building Fund. Mr. G. Tatman, hon. treasurer, introduced Mr. and Mrs. Spridgeon who performed the opening ceremony, and a delightful interlude followed when little Susan Hillier, aged four, presented a bouquet to Mrs. Spridgeon. The stalls included:—White Elephant, Fancy, Toilet, Flower, Fruit and Vegetable, Needlework, Home-made Cakes, Pound, Toys, and the Sunday School Stall, and Bran Tub for the children.

The social in the evening was appreciated by all, the entertainers being Mrs. Frost and Mr. C. Scott (soloists) and Barry Culley (elocutionist).

The proceeds, after all payments, amounted to £120, and the thanks of the Committee are due to all who helped in any way to make the event so successful. —A. W. S.

Attenborough Parish magazine

The first ten years saw the successful launching of many of the community groups that are still going strong. The Youth Club, a branch of the Mothers' Union and both Men's and Ladies groups were launched between 1954 and 1964. The 10th anniversary was celebrated at a harvest supper with tickets selling for 2/6d.[13]

Internal view of St Peter's before the building project

Reverend Robert Warburton was appointed in 1954 and served Attenborough Parish (including Toton) for many years. His farewell service was some 13 year later in July 1967. There has been a succession of curates, over the years. Included amongst them have been Reverends Lionel Boniface, Michael H Lumgair, Robert Hollingshust, Angus Parker and Peter Gibbs. Raymond Adair, an Irish Church Army Captain, was a much loved minister. He started the monthly pram service with his two children to encourage mothers and children and where noise could be allowed. It began a long tradition.

Pram Service 1979, Michael Lumgair playing the guitar

1990 was an important year for St Peter's. It marked the completion of phase one of the building project. A new porch was added and a permanent building replaced the hut at the rear; Bishop Patrick officially declared the new space open. St Peter's has been and still is an active church. It has a range of different groups under its umbrella and hosts a variety of events. The congregation has grown. A building project to extend and improve took place, an agreement with the Methodist church to work together and a group to support playgroups and youngsters in the form of Busy Bees pre-school are just some of the achievements of the church. Behind this site were the fields of Whyatt's Farm.

The St. Peter's Project.

WE'RE BUILDING:-

- A BIGGER CHURCH - We will be extending the church, and so increase our seating capacity to 240. The extended church will continue to be a multi-purpose hall, used for worship and available at other times to church and other community groups.
- A NEW BUILDING BEHIND THE CHURCH To replace the existing Back Hall. This will have five rooms, housing all our Sunday School Groups and creche during Sunday worship. The new building will include a kitchen/lounge area.

St Peter's Church 2012

[13] St Peter's Church -50 years of Worship

Whyatts Farm, & Street Lighting

Another collection of buildings long gone are those of Whyatt's Farm, noted as Sunnyside

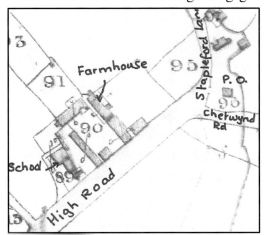

Farm in the 1930s,[14] which stood beside and behind Toton Endowed School. It was occupied during the 20th century by Bill Whyatt. Farms, were known by the name of their current resident. Bill Whyatt was renowned for a keeping a bull whose horn unfortunately blinded Bill's father (another Bill) who subsequently wore a patch over his eye. A small number of dairy cows were kept and, although there was a small dairy in the farm, in later years the churns were collected and taken elsewhere. A local resident remembers, in the 1950s, cows walking down the High road to and from milking. A milk bottle, discovered in a local garden, records the activities of such a dairy herd: W.Whyatt, Sunnyside Farm, Toton.

Bill (William) Whyatt, moved into the village around 1920, and became a prominent member of the village. He attended many Parish meetings and towards the end of the decade, was the Chairman of Toton Parish Council (1928). This body met in Toton Endowed School, during the 1920s, very handy for Bill.

The council discussed weighty

Farmhouse- Whyatt's Farm

matters like footpaths and lighting and who were to be the Overseers of the Poor. The earliest lighting applied for was two gas lamps. One was to be put near the entrance to Toton Fields and the other by Mr Hallam's farm. This proposal came in 1901 (whilst the council were still meeting in the vestry at Attenborough Church). Further lighting issues occurred in 1926 when two electric lights were to be erected – one at the corner of Stapleford Lane and one on

Barn at Whyatt's farm

Nottingham Road. These lights- 2 columns, with 60 watt bulbs, were to be used sparingly.

---

[14] Electoral roll 1935

The Minutes of the meeting stated *"-to be burning from one hour after sunset until midnight and from 4 a.m. until 1 hour before sunrise from 1st August to 15th May."*[15] A further lamp for Rutland Avenue was added in 1930.

The farm gradually declined. Its barns were used for storage. A local resident parked his vintage car in one, another local stored his pony and trap there, Hunt's nurseries used another barn for mushroom growing and a colony of bats roosted among the rafters. The farm was eventually demolished around 1960. Douglas Court, named after the son of the builders Taylor Bros, now stands on the site.

Opposite this site, are the house and bungalows between Rutland Avenue and Chetwynd Road. *"The bungalows either side of Rutland Avenue were owned by the Watson Brothers. One kept pigs and the other had a small butcher's shop in the garden. Rutland Avenue was rutted, had several wooden buildings, a large orchard and goats tethered in the middle of the road."* (Eileen Hall).

Rutland Ave

Developments in the 20th century have seen more side roads, such as Newland Close and Empingham Close. It has brought a variety of house styles, bringing individuality and uniqueness to Toton.

Chetwynd Road, former Turnpike Road also known as Main Road or Old Road
Chetwynd Road is a continuation of the High Road; made into a turnpike road between Long Eaton and Beeston in the 18th century and then disturnpiked in 1870. Chetwynd Road was bisected in 1915 when the National Shell Filling factory was constructed by Lord Chetwynd (a relative of the Birkin family) during the First World War. Gates were put across the road and though initially it was still used for residents it was considered too dangerous and the road was completely closed, for through traffic. At one time a special permit could be obtained. *"The road from Chilwell village carried straight on at depot corner. Up to 1939 a permit could be obtained to use the old road which connected to Chetwynd Road. Needless to say it was more trouble than it was worth leaving the way open for building."* (W Whyatt)

The Shell Filling factory, begun in 1915, was in full working operation within twelve months. By the time the war ended over 19,000,000 shells, 25,000 mines and thousands of large bombs had been manufactured and despatched. At the end of the war the factory was closed and the area declined. The War Office, in 1934, decided that mechanised transport should be centralised and therefore the land of the Shell Filling factory came back to life as the Central Ordnance Depot (C.O.D.) which expanded greatly during 1939 with the build-up for World War II.[16]

Marching out of C.O.D. led by the band

---

[15] Parish Meeting Minute book   PAC 80/1/1 Nottinghamshire Archives
[16] Chilwell Garrison

This large complex has had a profound effect on Toton. Workers from the factory in the mid 20ᵗʰ century streamed in and out of the gates on Chetwynd Road and Nottingham Road. Thousands of local people worked here.

"The Chilwell Depot was of course extremely busy during the war and for many years afterwards and since Chetwynd Road was one of the main entrances, I grew up with the sight and sound of heavy traffic and also soldiers marching up and down. I was however startled and, I think, a little afraid to be woken on one occasion just before my fifth birthday by much shouting and cheering and the blowing of bugles. My mother came into my room and said "The Wall's over", at least that was what I thought she said and I could not understand why everyone should be so excited because a wall had fallen over! Fortunately I had lived through all but the first nine months of the war without being aware of what was happening – it must have been very frightening for any child born just a few years earlier." (A.S.Taylor)

Another former resident of Chetwynd Road also remembers the work force streaming out of the gate at the end of a shift. *"Generally a quiet road, it was also one of the main entrances to Chilwell Depot. Four times a day the road became virtually one-way as the civilian work force streamed in or out. Most travelled by bike or foot – few cars. We could hear the bugle calls as we played outside, so we always knew when it was lunchtime, and we often heard the band practising. Once the band actually marched along the road, which was very exciting. One special day, we saw sand coloured vehicles including tanks, I think, rolling along the road, probably at the time of the Suez crisis. What lay beyond the gates at the end of the road was always a mystery."* (H.Knewstubb)

Miss Blackshaw and Juniors 1935

Old wooden classroom with outside toilets erected 1933

Chetwynd Road Primary School
The children of the army personnel attended (and still do) the nearest primary school, on Chetwynd Road. The nature of army life resulted in a constant change of pupil numbers at the school. The school, infant and junior, opened as Toton Council School on 24ᵗʰ April 1933, in two wooden classrooms with accommodation for 98 pupils as a result of the closure of Toton Endowed School.

In the school year 1935 - 1936, the number on roll has increased from 43 to 118, while the accommodation has accordingly been raised to 194 by the erection of a second hut. *The opening of the Army Transport Depot has been responsible for the rapid increase of numbers and the influx of children from different parts of the country and from abroad. High praise is due to the Infants teacher who although inspired by a real love for her work and possessing a natural gift for dealing with children, has a particularly onerous task in preparing for the Junior school, 51 pupils from 4 to 7 years of age. Well graded apparatus and early training in self reliance has combined to make this room a happy hive of industry, while the varied recreational activities are greatly enjoyed by the whole class.[17]*

Life was less complicated in the early and mid 20th century. Less technology meant that toys were simpler, hand-made or invented. Skipping, roller skating and riding on a scooter were enjoyed on the cul-de-sac that Chetwynd Road had become. Children would congregate at the school gate where *"there were some useful bars for balancing, somersaults and so on."* (H.Knewstubb)

Miss Day –Toton Council School.

"We had quite a large garden, both front and rear, so as a toddler I had plenty of space to play and a reasonable amount of toys, invariably second – hand or made of wood by an uncle or friend of my parents, but I spent a great deal of time standing just inside the front gate watching the traffic going to and from "The Depot" as we always called it. (There was actually a signpost on Stapleford Lane with an arm pointing down Chetwynd Road saying "To Depot"). I was quite an observant child and I soon began to notice the same people passing every day, mostly on foot or pedal cycle, but a few on motorbikes or auto-cycles. I also began to notice the registration numbers on vehicles and soon became aware that vehicles with two letters and four numbers, such as TV 5678 always looked older than those with three letters and three numbers, e.g. BTV 123, as indeed they were, as I discovered later.

There was also a grey-haired lady with a hat who rode by on a "sit-up-and-beg" cycle every day. She seemed to me (aged about four) to be quite elderly and I wondered what she did if she worked at The Depot. Later on, when I started school, I learned that she was Miss Catherine Day, who taught the infants class. She was only about forty years old and cycled from Attenborough. There was also a younger lady who rode her cycle rather more quickly –

Mrs Henson and her class 1947

this was Miss Lewis.

On May 28th 1945, the day after my 5th birthday, I was taken along to the school, just a few yards from my house and introduced to the, Headmistress Miss Wells, who took my details and then placed me in the infants class presided over by the

[17] Inspector's report 1936 in School Log Book

grey-haired lady with the cycle. (In those days, one did not apply for a place at a school, you just turned up and somehow they found a place for you.)

Chetwynd Road was remarkable in that not only did it cater for all the children in Toton aged 5-11, but also took in many army children who would appear from Singapore, Malta, Gibraltar and other exotic-sounding places, only to disappear just as suddenly as their fathers were posted away from Chilwell. Because of the large numbers of children and only four classrooms (until about 1949), the class sizes were inevitably large and it was not possible to move up on a yearly basis, but only as space became available. Nevertheless, it was a well-run school with few disciplinary or truancy problems. It expanded during my six years there and I was taught by Miss Day, Mrs Henson, Miss Heath, Miss Lewis, Mr Brooks, Mrs Croft and Mr Miller, but not Miss Wells, who retired and was replaced by Mr John Sutton around 1949. Mr Sutton was red-haired, red-faced, loud-voiced and in fact something of a bully, who terrified most of us, but he must have been well-thought of by the authorities, since he obtained the headship of the new Bispham Drive school in 1963". (A.S. Taylor)

Football team 1953, Mr J. Sutton Headmaster, Mr Gaskell Miller

Mr Gaskell Miller was a keen sportsman and ran the football team, which did have its own football strip although the children attending the school had no uniform, unlike many schools. There was no special clothing for P.E. or other sports. Uniform was not a common feature until much later.

Sports Day circa 1952, no P.E. clothing

One pupil has become famous in the folk singing world. Anne Briggs has written many songs, produced several CDs and is thought of with affection by many people. On leaving Chetwynd Road School, she attended Bramcote Hills Technical School (opened in 1955). Prior to the opening of this school and George Spencer, pupils from here often attended Grange Secondary School, Convent or the Grammar School in Long Eaton.

Anne Briggs CDs

This school, like many buildings in Toton, has been known by many titles – Chetwynd Road Primary School or Toton Council School, Toton Junior Mixed and Infant School, and, for a short time, Toton Infant school. It has been transformed with the addition of a hall, and replacement buildings. The school has grown in size from two classes to eleven.

It was also the only meeting place for the community until 1954. The Sunday School met here, as did the Brownies and Guides, Youth Club, Women's Guild, Civil Defence and the Coronation Committee. Groups planning to build their own halls met here and social occasions such as whist drives took place here. Over the years there have been events to mark Royal celebrations, with sports events, singing and concerts organised for these.

Infant block and computer suite 2008 Chetwynd Primary School

Fancy Dress competition Toton Council school

To celebrate the Coronation of Queen Elizabeth in 1953, there were many events to mark the occasion throughout the Urban District of Beeston and Stapleford. In Toton there were many events culminating in a Coronation Tea free to all children. An Arts exhibition was featured in the School which was open in the evenings for viewings. A fancy dress competition was organised. This was followed by a parade and a procession to the school. (Appendix 5)

Toton had a good reputation for organising. The King George VI Silver Jubilee Celebrations, in Toton, 1935, which featured the 'Yo Yo' band, parades, sports and singing, were deemed by the Stapleford and Sandiacre News (May 11th) to be the best organised. A similar promise of success was promoted in the Coronation Booklet *"June 6th will see celebration personified on Toton School Field, where a promise is given that a free tea will be given to children. Even if Toton does qualify for the smallest spot in the Urban District, it knows how to celebrate given the opportunity. Yes and on £70 too!!"*[1]

Chetwynd Road, is a pleasant mix of houses. New bungalows have been built where Chetwynd Nurseries (Hart's) once prospered.

Chetwynd Rd, old main rd, site of nurseries

At the edge of Toton, on the old main road just inside Chilwell, there was a Malthouse. The site is now occupied by the Sergeants' Mess in Chetwynd Barracks.

Malthouse

---

[1] Beeston & Stapleford UDC Coronation Festivities Book

A Stroll up Stapleford Lane – From the Post Office towards Stapleford.

In 1901 the walk up Stapleford Lane would have been very different from the scene that meets anyone today. A hundred years ago, there would have been only three buildings: the Blacksmiths, the Keeper's Cottage and Hill Farm between Chetwynd Road and Stapleford. A rural, agricultural landscape was the scene on view.

Toton Post office, alias Blacksmiths, alias Crockers', formerly Hoytes'

The blacksmith, an important man in an agrarian economy, would have looked after the

Toton post Office and shop

working horses and riding horses, of which there must have been a good number. The house, now number 2 Stapleford lane – Post Office and shop, was rented by the Eaton family for many years.

William Eaton moved with his wife and son to Toton from Stapleford around 1848, and his next two children, Margaret and William were born in Toton. The address, Odd House, may signify a detached house.

Addresses were not recorded during the 19th century, presumably because people knew where

1846 Rent book	1851 census	1861 census	1871 census	1881 census	1891 census	1901 census	1911 census
William Eaton blacksmith & grocer	William Eaton (33) blacksmith	William Eaton (43) blacksmith	William Eaton (52) blacksmith	William Eaton (63) blacksmith	William Eaton (73) blacksmith and farmer	William Eaton (81) No occupation	William Eaton (38) blacksmith
Plot 96	Attenborough	Odd House Toton	Cottage Toton	Toton	Toton Row	Main Road Toton	Stapleford Lane

everyone lived and there was no need to record obvious details. One therefore has to assume that the Eaton family stayed in the same house with the forge. The blacksmith, William Eaton (the younger) was still registered on the electoral roll as blacksmith in 1925. Sometime after that, with the growth of the motor car and decline in farming, the need for a blacksmith ended. The business became a Post Office and shop.

Mr Cyril Samuel Hoyte took over the corner shop in the 1930s. He applied for a licence to sell wines and was supported in his endeavour by a large proportion of Toton residents. A copy of the petition to support his application for the 1940/1941 licensing year still exists.[1]

COURTESY AND SATISFACTION
IS ASSURED AT

HOYTES STORES LTD.

Directors: J. E. TAYLOR, P. B. CHARLES

HIGH-CLASS GROCERIES
WINES and PROVISIONS
BEERS. CONFECTIONERY
DAILY DELIVERIES TO ALL PARTS
2, STAPLEFORD LANE, TOTON
Phone: Long Eaton 85.

NEWSAGENTS.

---

[1] C/PS/B/17/14 Petty Sessions- Nottinghamshire Archives

50

Ten years later it was a Mr John Eric Taylor, who was granted the licence and this time it included spirits.[2]

The Corner shop, after many name changes, is still thriving as a store and off licence and still includes the Post Office. Mr and Mrs Crocker retired after many years in the shop and the business transferred to another owner and has

Crockers alias Blacksmith, from Chetwynd Road

undergone more changes.

Mr & Mrs J Crocker, ran the shop for many years, stand here beside the post box c 2000

The Smithy has been a combined business for a long time. The Post Office (run at one time by Freda Walters) moved from the left hand side of the building to join the grocery business. The wines and spirits department once situated in a separate room at the back also merged within the main shop.

In the 19th century and earlier the pinfold, or pen for stray animals, was located next to the Smithy. This was a lucrative source of income for the landowners as far back as 1620 when presumably farmers had to pay to release their animals from the pinfold, much as modern drivers have to pay to release their cars from clamping.

Tel. : Long Eaton 85

Toton General Stores Ltd.

2, STAPLEFORD LANE, TOTON

GROCERIES, PROVISIONS
WINES, BEERS & SPIRITS
FREE HOUSE—All leading brands sold

The houses now situated on Stapleford lane from here to the modern traffic lights are a product of 20th century development. At first it was small scale development with individual plots bought and houses built. Holme Lea, 1 Stapleford Lane, was occupied Mr Albinson a local councillor, a retired teacher and also the School Manger. This was followed by other bungalows and houses in the 1920s and 1930s. The house is close to the bend whose sharpness was lessened in order to reduce accidents.

Eileen Hall remembers

"My father, Edwin Jacklin bought a piece of land from Mr Birkin, the lace and farming magnate, on Stapleford Lane around 1927. He built the bungalow known as no 11 Stapleford Lane but then called Allandale. He moved in with his wife Maud and daughters Stella and Eileen. Later he built the bungalow no 15 (not 13 as this is an unlucky number) but then called Hill View because across the road were fields and a clear view of the hill. Next door was Hunt's Nurseries (where Honiton Close is now). Then there was a small bungalow at no 25, with fields before White House and its grounds (now Blackrod Close.) The Travers family lived here. Mrs Travers being the daughter of Mr

Mr Edwin Jacklin

---

[2] PS/B/30/18 Off Licence – Nottinghamshire Archives

Chambers who founded the Chambers Cardboard factory. Barton's ran a bus service, from Ilkeston to Stanton-by-Dale, through Toton ending at Shardlow. Groceries, meat greengrocery, milk and bread were delivered by a horse and cart or bicycle. Pavements were kept spotlessly clean by a man with a broom and a barrow. Those were the days when everybody knew everybody else, turned too and helped in times of trouble and lived peaceful lives. All this changed with the war when Chilwell Depot was in full spate and all land seemed to be taken up with buildings to house workers. Alas, a village no longer."

The bungalows and houses were built on the flat alluvial land of the Trent floodplain. The land drains well and the soil is good. Maybe because the soil is light and well drained, it was such a good place for nurseries; the soil warms early, so producing plants early for sale. There were several nurseries in the area, most of which have been swallowed up by housing

Bungalow Stapleford Lane built 1927

developments. Eileen Hall is a prominent member of the community and her house and garden have over the years seen many events, meetings, gatherings, sales and garden parties. Many of these have raised significant amounts of money for a wide variety of charities as Eileen and her friends have tirelessly worked for others: the Leprosy Society, the Neonatal Baby Unit at the Queen's Medical centre, (knitting lots of woolly clothes) and Church of England Childrens' Society and Renal Unit at Nottingham City Hospital.

Stapleford Lane continued to have a feel of the countryside about it for a few more years. Fields still stretched upwards towards Stapleford.

Ernest Hall's memoirs

"My mother had always wanted to live in the country. She really hated living in the congestion of streets in towns. Spridgeons were building a lot of houses in Stapleford Lane, Toton and I was very keen to move (from Long Eaton). The detached house we all liked was 38 Stapleford Lane, then the last house on the right hand side until one at the top of the hill. This really well-built house was £600 with an additional £7 10s 0d for a good garden shed. I borrowed £515 at 5% interest repayable over 30 years at £2 18s monthly. It was a figure I could easily manage but had no intention of letting it go on for that time. I hated HP (Hire Purchase) of any sort.

It was a lovely lane, lime trees on either side of the road, Daykin's farm just a few yards up the road and Holland's farm just beyond us. There were fields at the back of us and ahead up the lane. Holland's Farm (Hill Farm) was away to our right, well away from the road. The cattle came right up to the fence and broke onto our lawn a few times. Walking down the lane, with the scent of the limes, birds singing, cow manure on the road, it really

was country. At the top of the hill, was a spinney and a bridle path to Chilwell whilst further on were Gregory's Rose Gardens and in the summer the fragrance and colour from these were almost overpowering.

Even in the Army at 2s 6d a day, I made an allowance home of 1s and 6d per day which was augmented by the Army so my parents easily managed also to live as well as they were allowed to in wartime with rations etc."

The 1920s was a time for expansion, not only of housing but of nurseries. There were several in Toton.

Hunt's Nurseries

Hunt's Nurseries

Hunt's Nurseries, also known as Toton Nurseries, was situated on Stapleford Lane. During the Second World War it had to increase production, so used the school playing fields on Chetwynd Road in addition to it's own land. Land girls worked here during the war and one of them fell in love and married the celebrity, author and cartoonist, Norman Thelwell. This nursery grew many salad crops and was well known for a special strain of lettuce. The greenhouses were situated on land behind Whyatt's Farm and some of the barns of this farm were used by the nursery for mushrooms at one time. A concrete greenhouse, one of the first of its kind, was erected here. Ken Hunt, the owner, moved eventually to another site in Leicestershire. He is also remembered for his fine tenor voice and his love of opera.[3]

Hart's (Acton's) Nursery situated at the end of Chetwynd Road had larger greenhouses than Hunt's. It was later to become Chetwynd Nurseries/Oasis with a base in the Co-op superstore. Birkin's Nursery covered a small plot behind Portland/Carrfield Road and finally at the top of Stapleford Lane was Gregory's Rose Garden. Other small nurseries and allotments utilised areas off Nottingham Road.

Toton was an agricultural community, with few skilled workers. Cobblers, upholsters and other trades were situated in Chilwell or Long Eaton, even though the craftsmen may have resided in Toton. Likewise there were few shops, so local people needed to visit nearby towns for many items. There was however in addition to 'Hoyte's', another grocery shop: the Co-op.

Cooperative Society

A Co-op shop was established; Branch number 26 was established on Stapleford Lane, at the corner of Hill View Road, in 1940. This was a time when the Co-operative Society shops were expanding in

Former co-op store now a private residence. Hill View road.

---

[3] Norman Lewis

the area. Branch Number 24 was at Depot Corner, in Chilwell, which opened with great ceremony in 1937 and, following the war, Branch number 30 opened (Chilwell 1953), followed by the last branch the society opened, number 32 on Woodstock Road, Toton, (1958.) All these shops were either grocery stores or grocery and butchery.[4] *I remember the Co-op grocery store on the corner of Hill View Road for its lovely wooden fittings and counters.- and you were served.* (E.Knewstubb) The building on Stapleford Lane closed, became a haberdashery and a dress shop for a while and has since been converted into a private residence.

Further up Stapleford Lane beyond The White House, built for William and Fanny Travers, (now Black Rod Close) a factory was built.

Chambers Factory 1920s

Chambers Cardboard Works – Chambers Packaging Company

William Travers, the son in law of Fanny Chambers, (owner) began Chambers Cardboard Works, followed by son Fred Chambers. There was a Cardboard/Packaging factory (often marked as Etonian Works on the maps), sandwiched amongst the houses on Stapleford Lane and Carrfield Avenue, since the early 1920s. The factory, demolished in 1998[5] after 70 years on the site, in Toton, began life in Long Eaton. It made cardboard coffins in the First World War, owing to a shortage of wooden ones.

The firm made a variety of boxes, any shape or size, varying from ones suitable for one ton of peas, to the smallest size possible. About 700 or 800 tons of boxes

Chambers factory c 1979

left the factory per week[6]. The company flourished, sold some of their land for housing and expanded. More buildings were added, the machinery and vehicles updated and, of course,

---

[4] Long Eaton Co-operative Society a centenary history 1868 -1968

[5] Long Eaton Advertiser 22/1/1998

[6] A. Hunt –former employee

the name changed, to Chambers Packaging Company. Houses were added to Carrfield Avenue and Stapleford Lane, which eventually surrounded the factory. Life was generally calm but occasionally unusual events occurred. *There was great excitement when one night some-one set fire to the factory and fire engines blocked the lane[7]*. In later decades, lorries still managed to move goods and equipment but further expansion was not deemed possible and so the factory closed. In a comment when discussing the future for the site, one councillor remarked that *"Chambers tried very hard to remedy the noise and disturbance but unfortunately not to Council officers' wishes."*

Chambers Packaging surrounded, beside Stapleford Lane 1987

As an aside, it may be interesting to note that the surname, 'Chambers', has been long connected with Toton. Not only is Thomas Chambers recorded as pledging his allegiance to James 1st in 1603 but Thomas Chambers (1598) Richard Chambers (1627 & 1637) served as Church Wardens, in St Mary's Attenborough. John Chambers of Toton, is recorded as serving as a Juror, at a local inquest into the death of John Malyn (1539) -*"who was in a drunken stupor and intended to cross the River Erewash near Toton, his feet slipped and he fell into the river and was drowned."* [8]

The Chambers factory was demolished and the land sold for housing. St George's estate was built.

End of an era 1998

New Beginnings 2001

[7] Eileen Hall
[8] Calendar of Inquests

Methodist Church

Another landmark on Stapleford Lane, is the Methodist Church. This was the second church to be built in Toton. As early as 1953 various fund raising events had been held with the idea of building a new church. Early services were held in the newly constructed Coronation Hall. *"Sunday October 24th (1954) was an important day for Methodism in Toton. On this day we commenced evening services in Toton.... The first service was a Harvest Festival. It rained heavily and loyal souls who had worked hard to make this beginning possible, could easily have added their tears of disappointment to the flood. But at the time for the service to commence one hundred and fifty people had assembled and our hearts were cheered again. Mark you, there was a certain 'freshness' about the service – the hall had no door and the wind had veered round until it was blowing directly into the hall."[9]*

A site, on Stapleford Lane, backing up to the warehouses of the Chilwell Ordnance Depot, was purchased in 1956 and fund raising continued. One item of note (among many) is the salvage fund. This resulted in the collection of 838 lbs of woollies, 21½ tons of clean newspapers, and 20 tons of magazines which raised £176.[10] Hard-working folk collected, sorted and stored the papers. Other volunteers laid the car park and, in later years, extended the facilities and laid out the gardens.

Reverend Leafe, with silver trowel, laid the Foundation Stone November 1962

A service led by Reverend Thorne, to mark the laying of the Foundation Stone, was held in November 1962. Building commenced during a cold snowy winter. The Methodist Church finally opened on 28th September 1963. Mrs Ruth Leighton (the first Superintendent at the Sunday School) performed the opening ceremony. After ceremoniously knocking three times on the outer door, she was handed the key by the architect and then, on entering, she handed the key to Reverend Edward Page, the Superintendent Minister. The cost of the church, around £17,000 was offset partly

Building commences, the frame for the east window erected

by the proceeds of the sale of Mount Tabor and Zion Churches (Long Eaton). In 1987, Toton Methodist Church joined together with St Peter's Church, Toton, to work together, united.

---

[9] Newsletter Long Eaton Methodist Circuit
[10] Order of Service at the Opening of Toton Methodist church.

The most striking feature of this modern building is the 18 foot high triangular west window. It has been repaired and replaced with high tech features, including double-glazing and electronic blinds, which ensure the interior of the church is filled with light but the worshippers are not dazzled.

Methodist Church 2012

Various events have been held over the years. The Kerygama singers gave a presentation one Easter; talks and meetings also take place here. Guides and Brownies and other youth groups are regular users along with Toton Ladies' Circle and others. Support has been give to many charities such as the Leprosy Mission, National Childrens' Home and Oxfam.

Toton Library

Set back from Stapleford lane, is the unassuming but important building housing Toton Library. This small single storey building, which opened in Spring 1954, houses a wide selection of books. It developed from its early days when it was just a book box, stored at someone's house which was changed by the County library service periodically. From there it was housed, for a short time, at the Kosie Cafe and then at the local school before the present building was opened on Stapleford Lane.

Toton Library 1955

Regular visits by groups of Infants from local schools enjoy browsing the books and listening to stories.

The library staff issued books many years ago, with each member of the library having their own small card envelope. A sheet inside

Toton Library interior

each book was stamped to record the date due back. Plastic library cards replaced these envelopes. Books however continued to be stamped. This has now been superseded in the 21st century, with technology to scan books when issued or returned. Modernisation has affected other areas too. The lovely oak wooden doors have gone, replaced by swing doors and roller shutters for security.

Art Deco style oak front door

The land at the rear of the Methodist Church, the houses and the library, was once farmland. Plots 80 and 84 (Pinfold Close part) on the 19th century survey were farmed by Richard Mould (Hill Farm). These fields were still green and pleasant, until the Central Ordnance Depot extended its operations in the preparation for the Second World War. Warehouses, to house heavy vehicles, were built by the War Department. Peace-time, too, brings changes and these buildings were demolished after the sale for a large superstore. It was sold by the Ministry of Defence, to the Co-operative Society in 1981 for £600,000.[1]

Co-op Superstore to Tesco.

Warehouses on Swiney Way prior to their sale

Plans proposed in 1982 for a superstore were not popular. There were many arguments against having such a large superstore in such a small village. Residents met, the Council discussed and, after several rejections on the grounds of traffic congestion and sewage overload, plans were amended and finally approved for a retail store, storage space, restaurant, and eight shop units together with a 519 space car park and a petrol station. The Co-op Superstore opened in 1983, providing employment, and becoming an asset to the area.

The small retail units at the easterly end of the superstore included a short-lived doll's house shop, pet shop, card shop and pharmacy.

In the 1990s a monthly Farmer's market selling fresh vegetables and other British produce, operated. This ceased

Co-op Superstore, 1987

at the turn of the century. Access to the Superstore was via an entrance off Swiney Way which had previously existed as an internal road, on Chilwell Ordnance Depot.

The £4 million Co-op was opened by Mr D Green, the manager and the Mayor of Broxtowe, Mrs A. Morris.[2] It covered an area of 128,000 sq feet. Change,

Tesco 2012- western end

modernisation and new 'brooms' continue to occur. Tesco, the large food giant, bought the Co-op building and opened on the same site, in 2003. A local resident, Eileen Hall, was invited to cut the ribbon on the grand opening. The small shops disappeared into the vast

---

[1] Sale advertisement Walker Watson Hanson kept by B& DLHS
[2] Scrapbook 21 Eileen Hall now with B&DLHS (Beeston & District Local History Society)

emporium of Tesco, with the pharmacy and travel agent being the last vestiges of that episode.

Back at the junction where Swiney Way meets Stapleford Lane and Banks Road, there are now traffic lights. The junction has been improved over the years, widened to

Tesco petrol station 2012

allow easier access for large lorries and the volume of traffic that now by-passes the village en route from Chilwell to Stapleford. In the latest improvement, a large stately Turkey Oak tree was felled, one of the few remaining large trees planted over a hundred years ago. Before this junction was created, there stood a lonely house known as the Keeper's Cottage or lodge.

Keepers cottage

A two storey house, known as Keepers Cottage, was probably built during the nineteenth century. It may have been the home for a game keeper, who patrolled the spinneys in Toton. In the 1901 and 1911 census, a Samuel Brailsford, (gamekeeper) lived on Stapleford Lane, Toton, possibly in this house. He, his wife Rhoda and ten children

Stately Oak

inhabited this cottage, which at that time had only five rooms. It must have been crowded, especially in the morning when they all set off for work. The eldest girls worked in the lace trade and the boys were farm labourers.

No. 142. Keeper's Lodge. Toton.

The last tenant, remembers a gothic front door which had shrapnel embedded in it. The house was demolished in the 1960s.

Behind Keeper's cottage was a wooden bungalow and shop where *"all kinds of wonderful sticky sweets" were sold*[13]. The wine gums were a speciality and helped one up the steep hill on the long walk to Stapleford. Mrs Shipman's, at one time, sold a diverse range of odd items. The shop had a huge window and Sarah Shipman, herself, was a reclusive character who liked to wear long black dresses in the Victorian style.[14]

As one progresses up the hill towards Stapleford, there are two service roads either side of the main road. These are products of the growth of housing in 1930s, 40s and 50s, with a little of the remnants of the old hedges and trees. The grassy strip has been planted with crocus bulbs in an effort to brighten up the area. In times gone by this part of Stapleford Lane was a rural

---

[13] Eileen Hall
[14] N.Lewis

track. *"Stapleford Lane was narrow and hedged with hawthorn and wild roses. Violets and primroses were in abundance. A colony of bats lived at the top of the hill."* (Eileen Hall) The land on the hill, to the east of Stapleford Lane, was also former farm land and *"in the winter, when it always seemed to snow, this became our sledging hill, with many happy hours spent sliding to the bottom and hauling our home-made sledges back to the top."* (A.S. Taylor) *(1950s)*

Hill Farm – Holland's farm – Toton farm

This is the farm that once occupied the site to the east of Stapleford Lane. Hill Farm, with the access opposite where Woodstock Road is now, became part of a large military establishment. Much of its land was taken by Lord Chetwynd to create the national Shell Filling factory in 1915. The site was then expanded to form the Chilwell Ordnance Depot and after the expansion in 1938 with preparation for war, the farmhouse became an Officers Mess. *"..Hill farm has not the amenities of HQ in such things as Billiards rooms, but nevertheless there is plenty of mild social activity....*[15] This mess, like the other Officers' Mess, had its own library, so life here might have had a more pleasant aspect than some war time service. *"Hill Farm stood at the bottom of the hill roughly where an old conifer still stands today. This tree can be seen when looking through the metal fence opposite Woodstock Road. New houses were erected, rising up Stapleford Hill, a narrow steep incline with no pavement edges either side and hawthorn hedges cutting off the fields from the track.* (R.Wyatt)

Holland's Farm, in the tenure of first John Holland and then later in the 1930s by Alf Holland, was noted for breeding Dartmoor ponies, for a short time. Holland's Farm in the early 20th century was reputed to be the largest of Toton's farms and covered the land from what is now Bardill's Garden Centre to Chetwynd Road. Indeed it is some of this land that was sold to the council for the building of Toton Council School in 1933.

View into former Ordnance Depot, the site of Hill farm

Some of the old field names remained for many years: 'Near Whitgrass,' 'Far Whitgrass', 'Crowtree close', 'Middle Flatt' and 'Middle Upper Flatt' giving clues as to the terrain and location of the fields. The farm was another mixed farm with pasture

---

[15] Chilwell 1939-1945

and arable fields. The farm bordered Stapleford and is the likely source of the wheat for Stapleford Hall and timber for its fires. The survey of 1802, states that "Sir John Borlas Warren is to keep the rights of Spinney"[16]. In 1822 the farm covered over 129 acres, smaller than at the end of the century. The buildings included house, yards, outbuildings fold yards and stackyards. Among the buildings was a pigeon loft or dovecote.[17] The fields were the same: Wit Grass, Far Wit Grass and Crow Tree Close.

Wheat, barley and oats were the main crops grown, whilst pasture for sheep and cows was another important aspect of the farming economy. When the land was sold in 1855, to Thomas Birkin, some tenants remained in situ.

MAN CHARGED WITH MURDER OF WOMAN (86)

A 31-YEAR-OLD Chilwell man appeared before Shire Hall Magistrates in Nottingham this morning charged with the murder of 86-year-old recluse Miss Alice Dickson.

Near the top of the hill was a lone house. *The last building going up and hidden by trees, was for many years the home of a very private lady the daughter of a Long Eaton doctor, Doctor Dickson. Sadly Miss Dickson was murdered one winter evening in 1978 as she fed the birds in her garden. Miss Alice Dickson was 86 years of age. A young man eventually owned up to this tragic event. She would be seen early morning walking down the hill in her long Bohemian outfits, a lover of wildlife keeping to herself. After her death her house fell victim to an arsonist, the land was sold and a few houses have since been built on it.* (R. Wyatt)

This lone house with its Welsh name, Beinnfidagh, was lived in by Miss Dickson for many years. This unfortunate lady, remembered for long, black garb seemingly from another era was well known in Toton and was fond of nature, spending money on bird food and squirrel food. A young fox cub even visited her in her home. She was a strict vegetarian and kept goats for milk to supplement her diet. She liked the natural way of life.

Continuing the journey north towards Stapleford, at the top of the hill were rose fields. The scent and colour of the fields of roses in June was wonderful. Charles Gregory (from Chilwell) began the development of roses and developed Gregory's Rose Gardens partly in Stapleford and partly in Toton. Many roses bred here won accolades around the world. Roses such as Grandpa Dickson (Presidents Trophy 1965), Fragrant Cloud (Presidents trophy 1964[18]), Blue Moon and Peace were much sought after. A local resident remembers spending some back-breaking weeks helping with the grafting of the roses. In the summer, Italians would come over and prepare the parent root-stock and then the temporary summer workers would push the sharpened point of the new shoot into the prepared slot. The two parts were then tied together, *"the hardest work I ever did."* Scratches from the thorns must have been inevitable.

---

[16] DD/WN/54-57 Survey of Toton held at Nottinghamshire Archives
[17] K. Scattergood
[18] Gregory's Rose catalogue Spring 1970

Stapleford Lane looking south to the power station 2012

"Stapleford Lane in 1947 was still a country lane; only Darley Avenue, Cleve Avenue and Spinney Crescent led off it. Behind Spinney Crescent stretched bluebell woods and fields belonging to the Co-op Farm. Further down, 'Black pad' so called because of the mud, now Banks Road, led to Toton Sidings." (E Knewstubb)

West of Stapleford Lane, the land slopes down to the River Erewash. Once farmland, it has become a large housing estate with two schools and a few shops. The 1960s, saw a huge increase in the number of roads and houses around Banks Road and Woodstock Road with yet another phase, which extended the housing in the 1980s, almost to Toton Sidings, leaving just a narrow corridor of green.

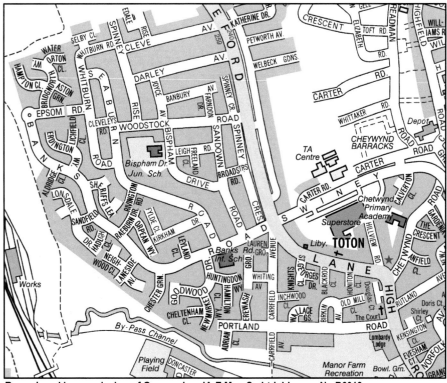

Reproduced by permission of Geographers'A-Z Map Co Ltd. Licence No B6019.
Crown Copyright 2012. All rights reserved. Licence Number 100017302

Field Farm/ Co-op Farm

The land to the west of Stapleford Lane was part of Field Farm or Co-op Farm, before the houses. Like the other farms, the size varied frequently due to the number of fields that were rented by the tenant or tenants. Access was from a track, now Banks Road, from Stapleford Lane. Another track led from behind Spinney Crescent, possibly to the osier beds.

Thomas Earp, among others, farmed part of this area which was sold in 1855, with the

View from Darley Ave over the last hay crop before building

Ploughing Co-op farm behind Spinney Crescent

rest of the estate, to Richard Birkin. In 1892 the area came up for sale again. The sitting tenant at that time was John Hallam who worked the mainly arable farm. The land was tilled and ploughed by horsepower. The farmhouse itself was another two storey building, in which two families lived (Morleys and Leesons in the 1930s). The farmhouse, barns, dairy and stables were close to the present Chester Green.

The Long Eaton Co-op Farm followed. It was mainly a dairy farm, specialising in Ayrshire cattle. Deliveries were by horse drawn vehicles, so horses and cows were as common, in the 1920s, as cars are today. The Co-op Farm was very extensive and at its height also rented fields adjacent to the Coneries Farm.

The Birkin family finally sold the land again in 1921 to the Long Eaton Cooperative Society. *"Toton Fields Farm comprising 120 acres or thereabouts – with farm house and useful buildings. The land is in excellent condition and suitable for market gardening."*[1] The land stretched from the Stapleford border to what is now Manor Recreation Ground. The Co-op themselves, were the first to develop an area for housing for the managers of Co-op properties and shops. A road was built parallel to Stapleford Lane and semi detached houses were built on what was to become Spinney Crescent.

Semi detached house Spinney Crescent

---

[1] Sale document DD546/9 Nottinghamshire Archives

These houses had views of one of the last spinneys in Toton, formerly a preserve of the chief landowner. Timber was needed and small game-birds, such as partridge, could be found here. (The last remaining spinney is at the top of Stapleford Lane adjacent, to a once thriving rose growing nursery.) The leafy woodland path through the spinney, where children lugged home logs for bonfire night, has now disappeared in a large housing estate. The wildlife that inhabited the spinney has also vanished.

Gradually during the 1920s and 1930s houses began to appear on Stapleford Lane. Houses were needed for the growing Chilwell Ordnance Depot and for people working in nearby towns. The 1950s saw a large development. In 1956 the Co-op sold their farms to a developer R Taylor of Attenborough and work began on the area between Banks Road and Woodstock Road. Banks road itself was constructed in the late 1950s. The spinney was cut down and houses on Banks Road covered the ground.

Spinney Wood

Banks Road houses, site of the Spinney

Various enterprises grew up around the Banks Road and Swiney Way junction. Frosts garage, a pharmacy and a shop (now a hairdresser's) were on three corners of this area. A doctor's surgery and some flats were added to Spinney Crescent in later years.

Frost's of Toton

L. Frost & Son (later to be Frost's of Toton) began life on Carrfield Avenue before Banks Road was built. Lesley Ivor Frost was an engineer who built up a business in one asbestos garage and one interconnecting wooden garage. These were accessed from 16a Carrfield Avenue, which had a long driveway. The land behind butted up to the track to Field's Farm. The business developed as

Frost's garage Banks Rd - petrol 37p a litre

the area developed. A new car showroom was built, the old garages demolished and new workshops built. The business crept onto Banks Road. Houses, now Lauren Grove, have replaced the old site. The business passed to the son, Brian Frost, and together with John Wright and Terry Sadler the business expanded, selling and repairing cars. The Opel range of cars was marketed before moving to Vauxhall cars.

Famous faces from television's Coronation Street, including Percy Sugden and Sally Webster, have visited. Promotional launches of new cars, have been celebrated with balloons and other festivities. Launches of Vauxhall cars such as the Nova, Astra and Cavalier have attracted many visitors to the showrooms.

Des Barnes (Coronation Street with John Wright

Launch of the Cavalier

Life has not always been rosy, however. The petrol strike (circa 1979) saw a 'Green Goddess' bringing fuel to Frost's forecourt petrol pumps.

Memories of pleasant service, and a reasonable price linger with former customers of this independent retailer. It was a sad day when the garage closed in 2000.

However life is transient and things move on. It is now a thriving Day Nursery and an asset to the community.

Percy Sugden (Coronation Street) pops in for a visit 1992

Close to this garage, is Banks Road Infant and Nursery School. This is the second of two schools opening in this area during the 1960s.

A 'Green Goddess' delivering petrol

New Schools

Banks Road Infant and Nursery School opened in 1966. It was a modern purpose built school. This single storey building sits comfortably and quietly beside Banks Road. In spring, the trees on the site, are a mass of beautiful colour, an attractive and inviting place to come

Banks Road Infant school 2010

to. The school has kept track with ever-changing educational trends benefitting from new technology, new ideas and modern equipment. An outdoor classroom has been created, which allows young children to explore and develop their physical and mental skills in a positive way.

Miss M. Smith, later becoming Mrs Jowett, was the first Head Teacher. She moved from the school on Chetwynd Road bringing her staff and Infant aged pupils. Miss M Smith organised her school curriculum to follow the 'Integrated Day'. She found it was suitable for her school and the children within it. *"We have been operating the 'Integrated Day'. This means that class teaching is largely abandoned and children are taught or advised individually or in small groups. In this way each child works*

Outdoor Learning area Banks road Infant school 2010

at his own level and is neither held back or rushed forward. The building and the furniture lend themselves to this form of education and the rooms are divided up into areas for Number, Writing, Handiwork etc and the divisions are changed according to need."[1] This new school, had its own kitchen with meals provided by the cook Mrs Goodall. At that time 60% of the children stayed for a hot meal.

The housing growth in the area has meant that this school flourished and grew. One of the first buildings on the new estate north of Banks Road, in the 1960s, was a junior school.

Bispham Drive Junior School was built in 1962, with Mr John Sutton as Headmaster, to replace the wooden huts of the Toton Mixed School on Chetwynd Road. The

Bispham Drive Junior School 1963

whole section of juniors, with many of the staff and Headmaster, moved in December, to this brand new school, with a hall, a dining room, kitchen and large fields for sport. It opened for business on 8th January 1963 with 189 children. Miss Lewis was the Chief Assistant, as she

---

[1] Terminal report Autumn term 1966 in Managers Minutes

had been before. It began life with appropriate furniture, with further additions of a potter's wheel, an electric kiln, a woodwork bench and a handicraft table. A piano was delivered

Mr John Sutton, Opening Ceremony

during the first week, a necessity for a Headmaster deeply involved with music. Initially five classrooms, Head Masters room, staffroom and kitchen were ready for use, although the plan was to accommodate 320 children, in eight classrooms.

The school, though was not officially opened with pomp and ceremony until May 1965, after an extension for new classrooms was completed and other teething problems were sorted out. The school was opened by Brigadier Ranson, Garrison Commander of Chilwell Ordnance Depot. The programme included official speeches, choral speaking by pupils and songs performed by the choir. This was followed by a tour of the school with childrens' work on show.

Mr Sutton and Brigadier Ranson visit the school library

Mr Sutton worked in Toton for twenty-six years before retiring. he continued to work hard for the district as a active councillor including a spell as Mayor of Broxtowe. He is remembered with respect and affection.

The School has continued to expand and develop. Various outdoor areas of interest include a maze, climbing frame and an environmental area with a pond.

The School was recently praised in the 2012 Ofsted report, which remarked that the standard at which the children leave the school is generally above average, particularly in reading. The school has also received a number of awards including: Healthy Schools Gold Award, Eco-Schools Silver Award, and a School's Achievement Award.[1] A diesel train has also been named after the school following a rail safety competition win.

Bispham Drive Junior School 2010

To serve the community in a different sphere, a pub was built on the corner of Bispham Drive and Sandown Road.

---

[1] Bispham Drive Junior School website

Other Side of the Moon.

This pub was built, along with the rest of the housing estate, in the 1960s. It commemorates space exploration. It was the time when the Russians were photographing the dark side of the moon, rockets were launched, and manned exploration of the moon began, culminating with the landing on the moon of Neil Armstrong in 1969. The pub closed about forty five years later and was demolished in 2006 for redevelopment. Houses now stand on Chestnut Place, the old pub site.

Other Side of the Moon, Sandown Road

Chestnut Place houses on the corner of Sandown Rd

Over the years the area has developed from a raw building site to a mature and pleasant residential area as houses and gardens mature. The row of shops on Woodstock Road have come and gone. New houses and roads have been added, leaving just a strip of green between the estate and Toton Sidings.

Woodstock Road

A main road into the estate with shops was planned in the 1950s. During the next decade, roads and houses grew quickly beginning with Woodstock,

fish & chip shop, computer business 2012

Seaburn and Epsom roads. The Co-op built another shop on Woodstock Road. Allied at one time to the Co-op was a garage, where co-op stamps could be collected, a development from the dividend scheme. Advertisements show another change: the telephone number is a Long Eaton number which reflects the number of telephone exchanges that were in existence. Nowadays the Nottingham number 0115 extends over a very wide area from Long Eaton to Ilkeston (both Derbyshire geographically) as well many other suburbs in Nottingham. The Terence Davies Garage, a Datsun garage, was replaced by Toton Autos and that too has now disappeared in the march of progress. A fish and chip shop still remains close to a computer business and a mini supermarket, a convenience store.

Toton Sidings

The western boundary of Toton, is with Long Eaton, Derbyshire. It is here, at the southern end of the Yorkshire and Nottinghamshire coalfields, that Toton Sidings was created in the mid-nineteenth century. There was a great demand for coal in Victorian England, for domestic hearths and for industry. The collieries were churning out tons of coal and needed space where the wagons could be sorted and sent to their various destinations. Toton Sidings were established by 1856 and continued to grow rapidly. In the 1860s they were extended with the addition of a locomotive depot. [4]

A new industry with new jobs grew up. Thousands of people worked at Toton Sidings. Most of the workforce lived in Long Eaton but a few lived in Toton village or in the lodgings at the Sidings. These were manual workers, the majority of whom were born elsewhere. The census records show the birthplace of the workforce as varied as Norfolk to Notts and Leicestershire to Lincolnshire with the odd one from as far afield as Darlington (Durham).

Analysis and extracts from Census data			
1891	**Railway Residences & Occupations (some)**		**Place of birth**
Dowse Morriss	Railways Sidings	Horse keeper on railway	Lincs, Swineshead
Samuel Smith	Railway Sidings	Railway Guard	Northampton
Thomas Buggins	Railway Sidings	Railway Engine fitter	Bromsgrove
William Barnet	Railway Sidings	Railway servant	Oxon, Cropedy
Alfred Payne	Railway Sidings	Horse Driver	Bristol
Lewis Thornhill	Railway Sidings	Railway messenger	Gloucs, Cowley
John Shrewsbury	Railway Sidings	Horse keeper	Notts, Chilwell
1881			
George Barnes	Gate House Toton	Railway labourer	Ratcliffe on Soar
William Roe	Toton	Railway Waggon builder	Notts, Kimberley
George Pritchett	Toton	Railway plate layer	Notts, Granby
William Ellender	Toton	Railway labourer	Norfolk, Whissonett
Henry Bailey	Toton	Railway Goods Guard	Northants Hardington
Thomas Cartwright	Toton	Railway signalman	Leics Shepshed
Thomas Bower	Toton	Railway wagon repairer	Derbys Westwood –Weston Underwood?
William Moore	Railway Sidings	Railway wagon Chalk?er	Gloucester Arlington
Samuel Smith	Railway Sidings	Railway Goods Guard	Northampton
Joseph Osborne	Railway Sidings	Engine cleaner	Lincs, Market Deeping
Henry Tingay	Railway Sidings	Signalman	Huntingon, Brompton
Joseph Milward	Railway Sidings	Horse Driver	Bucks, Newton Blossomville
Samuel Walker	Railway Sidings	Engine Driver	Notts, Kimberley
1871			
Thomas Cartwright	Cottage , Toton	Signalman	Notts, Toton
James Booth	Toton Sidings	Rail Pointsman	Cambs, Isle of Ely

Horses were used extensively in the early years to move the wagons. *"In summer (1883) perhaps 30 or 40 shunting horses will suffice, but in a severe winter the grease in the axle box will freeze hard, the wheels instead of turning round will skid along the rails and two or three horses will be required to a single wagon. It is very interesting to see the sagacity of the horses picking their way among the moving wagons....."* [5]

---

[4] Memories of Working at Toton Sidings and Beyond.
[5] Toton Yards and the Erewash valley

Before mechanisation, gangs of men with long wooden poles lifted the connecting links between wagons, enabling locomotive shunters to move groups or individual wagons around the yards. In this way trains could be assembled to deliver coal to where it was needed. Steam engines were for many years the motive power of the railways. The yards were a hive of industry. The Sidings continued to expand and thousands of trains were assembled here, carrying the goods, particularly coal, to all parts of England.

Increasing traffic made modernisation essential as increased efficiency was needed to handle the huge numbers of loaded and empty wagons that passed through the yards.

A Fowler 4-4-0 2P Class Loco at rest c1959

Control Tower, North Receiving Sidings

Full mechanical 'hump' shunting was introduced in the 1930s on the 'Down' side. Building work to raise the hump by several feet took place to enable wagons to be shunted, by gravity, into the sidings, which were arranged in numerous fans according to destination. The hump operator set the route for a particular siding according to the chalk numbers on the wagons. This information was transmitted to the control tower which operated the brakes and points. This system, completed in May 1939, speeded up the movement of wagons considerably. Mechanisation of the 'Up' side was completed in 1951, necessitating the reduction in the hillside to increase the land for rails.

Toton became the largest marshalling yards in Europe, with about 1 million wagons passing through, per annum, at its peak in the 1960s. Thousands of people worked at Toton Sidings during this period. Coal, iron ore, steel and concrete pipes from Stanton Ironworks have all passed through the yards. Improvements in efficiency, diesel engines replaced steam engines, improved technology, computerisation and changing markets have led to a small workforce.

Closures of collieries and Corby steelworks significantly reduced traffic and therefore the hump sidings closed (1978 'Down' Sidings, 1984 'Up' Sidings).[6] The giant has shrunk.

The noise has gone. Crashing and

Kitson Dock Shunter 0-4-0ST &0-6-0 tank engine c1959

---

[6] Memories of Working at Toton Sidings and Beyond.

banging from shunting operations and whistling from engines, particularly on New Year's Eve, has ceased. Today the number of trains is smaller and buildings lay empty. Nature is encroaching.

Toton Fields Local Nature Reserve

This green space between Long Eaton and Toton is a linear strip of land running alongside the River Erewash, incorporating parts of Toton Manor Recreation Ground and some margins in Toton Sidings. It is managed by Friends of Toton Fields and Nottinghamshire Wildlife Trust but owned by Broxtowe Council. It was

Grasses & wildflowers inhabit the slopes & edges of Toton Sidings

opened in 2009 by the then Mayor, Councillor John Longdon. More than 100 local residents attended this event which was held at the Greenwood Community Centre.

Willowherb and Russian Vine scramble over neglected land

The site (sixteen hectares) includes several different types of habitat: two river channels, wetland, scrub and rough grassland, woodland planted during the last twenty years, old hedgerows, disused railway sidings, playing fields and maintained grassland. An inspiring sighting occurred in 2011 with sightings of water voles. After an absence of many years these little creatures were spotted in April, an encouraging sign to the management group.

Bird and bat boxes have been erected by the Friends of Toton Fields in the hope of bringing in more species, to recover what has been lost and create a diversity of life which will sustain wildlife and bring pleasure to the thousands of people who live within reach of this zone.

In this small area a variety of birds have been seen and recorded. Among others attractive long tailed tits can be seen with their distinctive tails flitting among the bushes beside the River Erewash. In May 2008 there were 37 species present, including whitethroats, willow warblers and our familiar robin.[7] (see appendix 5)

Melilot

The area is full of interest: over one hundred species of birds and over two hundred species of wild flowers have been recorded. The flora of this small area is varied, from colourful colonisations of the industrial margins, such as willowherb and evening primrose, to designated hedge margins planted with native wild flowers, the work of the Friends of Toton Fields.

[7] Friends of Toton Fields Records online

Bee nose down in a late spear thistle , September 2012

Trees are being established, with pines, rowan, willow and birch amongst the more common.

There are many access points, with bridges over the River Erewash from Long Eaton and various entrances in Toton, one of which is beside the new Greenwood Community Centre, Chester Green, close to the site of the original Toton Fields Farmhouse. This small multi-purpose building was built circa 1991 and is used by several local community groups, including Scout and Beaver groups and an over 50s group.

Greenwood Community Centre from the rear 2012

Close by is Banks Road, which takes its name from the bank of the stream that used to flow alongside the former track. As with many other streams in the area and indeed the Erewash today, the banks are steep in places. The stream has now dried up but Banks Road commemorates the past.

The stream flowed at one time near the junction with Carrfield Avenue, before flowing to join the River Erewash. This stream was a playground for small boys searching for 'treasure'. Life in the 1950s was less technological than the 1990s and the present day. Play involved looking for tiddlers (small fish) and tadpoles or, maybe, even newts. It involved climbing trees, finding conkers and battling to become the Conker Champion.

Searching the stream at the top of Carrfield Avenue.

Carrfield Avenue is a handy place for access to this green corridor. Its name also reflects the history of the area. Carrfield Avenue itself is split: half in Long Eaton and half in Toton. The name is thought to derive from "Carr Fields" mentioned in the parish awards of Long Eaton, there being at one time a Great Carr Field and a Little Carr Field. The word Carr or Karr is probably a Norse word meaning marshy. It is interesting to note that the field names covering the Toton side of Carrfield Avenue, were called Little Rice and Great Rice and the area between the two Erewash channels were called First Park and

Carrfield Ave looking towards Stapleford, 2012

Second Park. As the people who bought the land in 1904, were from Long Eaton, it is the Long Eaton name that is remembered.[8]

Number 80, Carrfield Avenue, adjacent to the junction with Portland Road, was a grocer's shop for many years known as Davidson's. During the late 1940s, when it was a chip shop, an extra treat was sometimes enjoyed, crisps. Potato crisps were sometimes made there, as there were no bags commercially available at that time.

Front of 80 Carrfield Rd, a modern comfortable house

"There was a shop on the corner of Carrfeld Avenue. This shop run by the Davidsons, varied between a grocery, greengrocery and chip shop. This achieved a certain notoriety around 1953, when one of the Davidson family fatally stabbed his brother–in-law Mr Wakefield, after a family argument. The shop eventually became a ladies hairdressers and closed many years ago."
(A.S,Taylor)

Carrfield Avenue began to develop in the 1930s with a clutch of semi-detached houses, a local builder, Edgar Walters, being heavily involved. House building has continued behind on former farmland (Erewash Grove); infilling has also taken place in many gaps. The entrance to Chambers Factory is now just another cul-de-sac, Ambrose Court. Close to Whiting Avenue is a motor repair shop, sited where a former lime pit existed, the lime being used in the construction business.

Rear of 80 Carrfield Rd as a Chip shop with the metal chimney attached to the side.

There still is another shop on the other end of Carrfield Avenue, with its own capacious car park. This too has seen changes: once known as Lees, it is currently a hairdressers'.

Hairdressers and Carrfield Ave

Portland Road crosses Carrfield Avenue and links it to Stapleford Lane, so there is a choice of access routes, unlike some modern roads.

Portland Road

Following the sale in 1921 of the estate, houses gradually began to be built along Portland road and the road itself developed. Semi detached house and bungalows were built during the 1920s and 1930s, with more development and side roads in the 1950s. Council Houses were built on Old Mill Close, in the 1950s, the name reflecting and reminding residents of the once important mill.

---

[8] Long Eaton and Sawley Archive online

The 1885 map shows Portland Road as a track leading down to the flour mill.

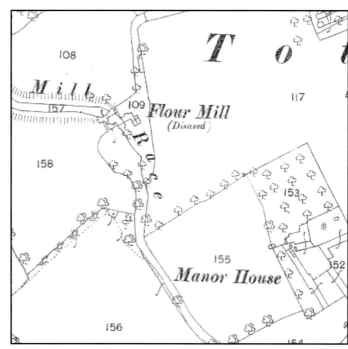

This mill, which must have been a substantial building judging by its shape, ceased grinding corn when cheap American imports of corn were allowed into Britain in the late 19th century. It became uneconomic to run a mill, as small as Toton's mill would have been.

Birkin Avenue, off Portland Road, commemorates the past in its name. It honours the Birkin family who owned Toton Manor between 1855 and 1921. Richard Birkin was a lace magnate and three times Mayor of Nottingham. Other members of the Birkin family have also been involved with the village in philanthropic and commercial ventures, Thomas Isaac Birkin being involved with supporting road widening and bridge schemes, as well as being involved with Toton Sidings. Many residents can cite the Birkin family on their house deeds.

Portland Road today has a mixture of styles and periods. Residential buildings and community buildings grace the landscape. Various local builders have lived along this road.

Birkin Avenue, off Portland Road c1951

Whitings (builders) set up a small business here for a while. They occupied the site of the kennels owned by Pinders in the 1930s. Mrs Pinder was well known for keeping wire haired fox terriers[9]. Greyhounds were also housed in kennels and raced at the nearby Greyhound Stadium, Long Eaton.[10]

Modern housing Portland Road.

Memories of strings of greyhounds on leashes being walked through the village still exist. Flats occupy the site of these former enterprises.

---

[9] K.Scattergood
[10] Eileen Hall

Allotments and nurseries have enjoyed using the fertile soil but these too have now gone under oceans of brick and mortar. Prize chrysanthemums were one of the items grown and shown by allotment holder Eric Harrison.

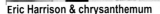

Eric Harrison & chrysanthemum

Coronation Hall

The 1950s were a boom time for buildings. Many village halls date to this era. Toton's, named because of the Coronation of Queen Elizabeth II in 1953 (when the Foundation Stone was laid), reflects the determination of local people. It was built by hand by the people of Toton after the Second World War. Twin foundation stones were laid in 1953 and then work began in earnest, aided by the odd ice-cream. Cyril Holmes (joiner) and Edgar Walters (plasterer and builder) worked tirelessly together with other voluntary labour utilising skill and time given by the people of Toton. They worked on the buildings in their spare time, particularly at weekends. The cost of the hall was £3000. The Council, who owned the land, supported the venture; *"the unanimous support of the Council*

Laying a Foundation Stone 1953

who considered it proper to give them a very long lease at a nominal rent and a guarantee of a loan for the building of Coronation Hall. We should not have done that if we had not been sure that at Toton there were a body of men and women prepared to see this thing through "Mr Redmayne, the M.P for Rushcliffe, stated that the people of Toton were public spirited and had come forward in the face of great difficulties and had striven to overcome them[11]. (Toton was within Rushcliffe Parliamentary division, so Mr Redmayne was the Member of Parliament for Toton).

Coronation Hall has been well used by the whole community. The local Primary School used it in the 1950s and 1960s as they had no school hall. Christmas concerts were held here. For a period of time class music lessons were also conducted here, with the children walking and carrying their percussion instruments. Woe betide anyone who

Locals prepare the ground

Work in progress

Cyril Holmes & partner up aloft

[11] Nottingham Journal 15.6.1953

75

left their triangle behind.

Other groups such as Brownies moved out of the school building, out of the old classrooms and into a this new purpose-built hall.

Sunday School Christmas Concert 1955

The Methodist Church held services here and ran a Sunday school here until their premises were built. They held social gatherings fund-raising events, meetings and concerts. Both the local school and the Methodist Sunday school held Christmas concerts.

19.12.1955 Today the school held its Christmas Concert. As in other years each class provided items for the remainder of the school and since we were able to use the Coronation Hall the items followed each other with a greater rapidity, were heard better and appreciated more than in other years and the space provided greater scope and opportunity. The concert was completed by midday.[12]

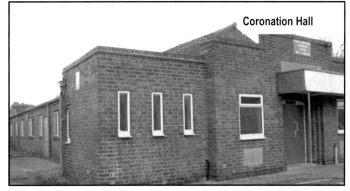
Coronation Hall

Other concerts followed. The 2nd Toton Brownies presented Dick Whittington on 25th January 1990 at 6.15p.m. The music was performed with one violin and three descant recorders: Nicola Trought, Nikki Barker, Louise Normansell, Rebecca Nicol. The singers were the whole Brownie pack and the characters included Fitzwarren, his daughter Alice, a clerk, a cook, ship's captain and of course Dick Whittington, his cat and pirates. Some doubling-up of roles was necessary and a lot of hard work went into the production.

Many groups have used the facilities in Coronation Hall over the years, including Toton Conservative Association, residents' meetings, playgroups, and senior citizens groups, to name but a few. Dances and other social events such as autumn fairs, concerts, meetings, lunches and various celebrations have all taken place in this busy, well supported community hall.

THANK YOU
for your patronage—we hope you have enjoyed a wonderful evening
May we remind you that Old Time Dances are held each Thursday with Mr. and Mrs. Grebby as M.C.'s and Mrs. Hay's Band
Admission 2/-

Toton Coronation Hall
Valentine Ball
Friday, February 17th, 1956,
8 p.m. to 12 Midnight.

M.Cs.
Mr Ken Hunt,
Mr. and Mrs. Ken Grebby.

Licensed Bar
(applied for)
PRIZES
CARNIVALITIES.

3/6

---

[12] School Log book

Fetes and gymkhanas were held on Manor Farm Recreation Ground in the 1960s. These were organised by the Joint Extension Fund Committee which was formed to aid the improvement of both the Coronation Hall and St Peter's. This committee had members from both buildings and helped to heal the rift caused after building two rival halls in the same year.[13] These Whit Monday events were well attended and included fancy dress competitions, stalls and music. On one occasion Long Eaton Salvation Army Band entertained the crowds.

Whit Monday fete 1960s

GYMKHANA.—The Church would like to record its warm thanks to Mr. Davison, the proprietor of the St. Leonard's Riding School, and all his helpers, for the excellent display which was held on Whit Monday. The queues waiting to enter the ground early on Monday afternoon were a tribute to the work of the Gymkhana Committee. The display by the Long Eaton Weight-Lifting Club and the Scout Camp Fire were a fitting climax to the whole programme. The profits of the day have been divided equally to assist the funds of the Toton Coronation Hall and St. Peter's Hall Church.

Lombardy lodge

This modern complex (1986) close to Coronation Hall, provides sheltered accommodation for the elderly, overlooking the Manor Park. It contains 41 flats and has the services of a warden who organises various events and classes. It has also been used as a Polling Station. This duty has been passed around available buildings. Polling stations previously held on Chetwynd Road in the school, have transferred to Lombardy Lodge, reducing the number of days lost for education.

Site of Lombardy Lodge

Lombardy Lodge

[13] St Peter's Church 50 Years of Worship and Witness

Nottingham Road

The current main Nottingham Road is a 20th century development. Following the closure of Chetwynd Road as a thoroughfare, this new road was built, joining up with Attenborough Lane before going into Chilwell. Houses began to be built from Toton Corner in the 1920s.

Long garden Nottingham Road

Those on the northern side had (and still have) long gardens, their long drives, trees and gardens giving a fair degree of privacy and seclusion. Mr Alfred Woodforth (pattern-maker by trade) lived in one of these. He was another *"grand old character"*[1] who became a talented woodcarver in later life He was involved with the community in many ways. He ran the Sunday School for Toton, was Clerk of the Parish Council and a Manager of Toton Primary School.

In the 20th century, various changes to the bridges (Erewash bridge, Toton Arches) and roads have taken place. *"Through the generosity of Sir T.I. Birkin a dangerous corner in the road was abolished and through the work and assistance of the Road Board a great improvement was made in widening and straightening the road in four places. Since that time the old turnpike road from Chilwell to Nottingham has been obstructed and a wide road made from Attenborough Lane to Toton with railway bridge over."*[2]

This railway bridge was known as Chilwell Viaduct or Depot Bridge. As the main road to Nottingham, it was in constant use by civilian traffic until it was demolished in 1989. It was the route used by Janet Davison who rode ponies bareback on the way to the blacksmiths in Beeston (Horace Wood, Wollaton Road). She remembers feeling scared as she rode over it, in case tanks came out underneath her and frightened her pony. Fortunately nothing ever happened-but the feeling remained.

Chilwell Viaduct 1989 looking the huts inside the Depot

Many people can remember battalions of men marching through the gates and tanks trundling up and down the roads. The tanks which used to trundle over the viaduct to the army base have long since gone. Much of the M.O.D. land has been sold. Further along Nottingham are two pairs of cottages, once called Toton Row.

---

[1] Obituary- unknown newspaper
[2] Then and Now

Toton Row - Rose Cottage

This pair of cottages, possibly built at the end of the eighteenth century, have been altered and modernised over the years by many owners. Rose Cottage (312 & 314 Nottingham Road) is now one house but was built around 1800 as two cottages. It was occupied in the 19th century by two families, who were labourers for nearby farms or for the railway. In the 1846 survey Rose cottage was plot 144 and 145 and occupied by Thomas Ellender and S.Smith. These families are recorded in the census documents that follow as residents of Toton Row.

Thomas Ellender, like others in Toton, was not born in Toton. He came with his wife from Norfolk around 1853 and settled in Toton where he stayed for the rest of his life, bringing up a family, who worked on the land or in nearby factories. Industrialisation was growing quickly in the 19th century and life was changing. Children were more likely to attend school in the later part of this century. The Ellender family show the change from agricultural occupations to industrial ones.

1851	Thomas Ellender birth Norfolk 1816	Agricultural worker	Married but not with family
1861	Thomas Ellender	Agricultural worker	Wife Mary born Norfolk
	William Ellender born 1847 Norfolk	Factory boy	Aged 14
	George Ellender birth 1849 Norfolk	Factory boy	Aged 12
	Sarah, Mary & John born Toton	At home	Aged 5, 4 and 2
1871	Thomas Ellender	Agricultural worker	Wife Mary
	Sarah and Mary	Mill Hands	Aged 15 and 14
	John and Eliza born Toton	Scholars	Aged 12 and 10
1881	Thomas Ellender	Agricultural worker	Wife Mary
	William Ellender	Railway worker	Aged 34
	John Ellender	Railway labourer	Aged 22
1891	Thomas Ellender	Agricultural worker	Wife Mary
Children have all left, the address is given as Toton Row. 1901 Thomas and Mary still in Toton Row.				

Rose Cottage 2012

Rose Cottage circa 1912

Rose Cottage, became occupied by two different families in the 1930s, namely Henson and Bliss[3]. Walter Bliss was yet another nurseryman, working and selling produce from allotments behind the houses. Following their departure, the Jacksons, market gardeners from Melbourne, moved in. Charles Pillmore, a landscape gardener and nurseryman, also lived in the area, just storing his equipment and parking his lorries behind Toton Row.

---

[3] Electoral Roll 1937 Directory 1940s

Toton Row - Long Cottage (304 & 306 Nottingham Road)

The auction sale particulars describe the building as "*Lot 1 Pair semi-detached cottages and gardens, with long frontage to Attenborough lane, near Chilwell Works*".[4] This cottage, like Rose Cottage, was originally designed for two families. It was extended around 1880 with an additional cottage being

Pillmore's lorry crashes into garden wall 306 Nottingham Road- Long Cottage c1940

tacked on the end. Since then more additions to the rear have allowed for a more comfortable living arrangement. A kitchen and internal toilet were added in the late 1940s. The original toilet was a small brick building in the garden. There was also a coal house which was needed as there was no central heating until the mid to late 20th century. There has been speculation, from looking at the brickwork, that it was once a single storey building,

The western end was a stable, which later became a kitchen. This was demolished in the late 1950s but has been replaced with another single- storey, structure. A later garage replaced a lean-to building, is attached to the eastern end of the building.

Long Cottage early 20th century

The Clarke family moved in (from the High Road) to 304 Toton Row, during the 1920s. The son-in-law, Ernest Rooke, a joiner, who worked in Long Eaton modernised and improved the cottage some twenty years later. The cottages were then converted into one dwelling in the 1950s. Large internal beams add to the character of the cottage. The 1940s and 50s were a period of austerity, following the struggles during the War. Toys were simple and often hand- made.

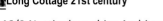
Long Cottage 21st century

Wooden bricks made by Dad

[4] Toton auction sale 1921 DD/546/9 Nottinghamshire Archives

80

The outlook over the floodplain and water meadows of the River Erewash has changed over the centuries. The river has been diverted, away from the road and straightened. It now wanders through the picturesque Nature Reserve.

Long Cottage circa 1912

The land behind these cottages, is no longer farmland or allotment, but is occupied by a modern housing estate created by the builders, Westerman, around the 1980s.

Army Influence

Further up the road, Thompson the greengrocer, lived in a 20th century bungalow. Charles Herbert (known as Bert) (294 Nottingham Rd[5]) grew and sold some produce from his land, and delivered some by pony and cart. This stock was augmented by fruit bought from a Nottingham wholesaler. The pony, 'Peggy', grazed in a nearby field when not working. Following this enterprise, a mushroom farm was developed by a Polish gentleman. These were grown in various army Nissen huts acquired after the Second World War.

The Parish boundary now follows the boundary of Thompson's property as the Chilwell Ordnance Depot incorporated land in the 1930s, and built more extensive rail links. Chilwell Retail Park now stands where once there were tank testing grounds. These testing grounds, with their man-made hills and dips, were used to test the engines. Tanks could be heard racing round and engines would often backfire sounding rather like gunfire. *"Mostly it was exciting but some of the bangs were frightening to a small boy"*. (N. Lewis)

"Tanks from the Chilwell Depot practised flame throwing from the tanks over little hillocks where Matalan is now. That was a bit scary. I hoped the flames did not come over the hedge." (local resident)

Chilwell Ordnance Depot 1943

Pillboxes, built as defensive gun emplacements for the Second World War, remained for some time. Various concrete structures were scattered around Toton. One was situated next to Thompson's by the Depot. Another one was on Miss Dickson's land by the corner of the wood, on Stapleford Lane.

---

[5] Electoral Roll 1937

Prior to the tanks, the land was agricultural and mostly grazing land. *"The more distant grazing fields some 1 ½ miles along the main road to Nottingham are now part of a large industrial estate. George would be hard pressed these days to drive his cows along there! The old Chilwell road bridge with its railway lines underneath into Chilwell depot has been levelled and now sports a galaxy of traffic lights."* (W H Roe, Limes Farm)

The reduction in military establishments led to the land being sold and the retail and industrial parks being developed. The sewage farm built, in the late 1920s, has had many

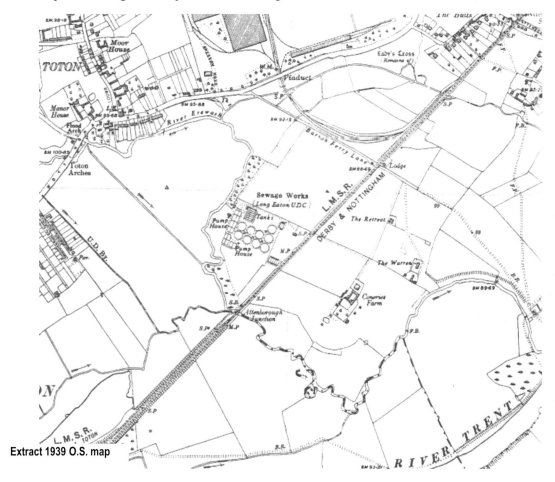

Extract 1939 O.S. map

upgrades to accommodate the number of new buildings that have been built in Toton and Chilwell. It sits quietly behind the Retail Park beside the lagoons and the railway.

The gate house for the railway level crossing gates was built during the latter half of the nineteenth century, where the railway crosses Barton Lane. It was often the duty of the wife of the family to work the level crossing gates whilst the husband worked elsewhere. This is indeed the case with Mr and Mrs Spurr and before them Mr and Mrs Spooner, with Mr Spooner being a Ganger Platelayer.[6]

The duties of the level crossing lady did not give her much time for chores such as shopping. It was on occasions such as these that local residents helped out. One such local lad remembers his time helping the gate keeper's wife in the 1960s. Nowadays a single barrier electronically operates and controls the traffic.

---

[6] 1911 census

BARTON LANE CROSSING. REMINISCENSES OF A PART TIME CROSSING KEEPER

After leaving school, and before going to college, I worked for British Rail for a year. I later rejoined BR, which began a lifetime working in the rail industry.

I started work in September 1965 as a porter at Attenborough Station, at that time a fully staffed station. Trent Power Signal Box opened about a year later, but in 1965 the signalling system was the old fashioned type, with signal boxes and semaphore signals, the same system that had been in use for over a century.

Barton Lane level Crossing

Mid-way between Attenborough and Trent Junction was Barton Lane Crossing. This lane ran from Nottingham Road to the river, and was mainly used by fishermen and the residents of a farm. By this time, Barton Ferry had ceased to operate.

Once Trent Power Box opened, the level crossing on Barton Lane became an automated half-barrier crossing, but until then was a hand-operated gated crossing. Gates were kept closed and padlocked against road traffic, and were only opened as required. Traffic was light, but might appear at any time, day or night. For this reason, a crossing keeper's cottage had been built by the Midland Railway sometime in the 19th century (date unknown). Here lived the crossing keeper, whose job it was to open the gates as necessary. It was normal practice for such cottages to be provided rent free, with the head of the household (male) being employed locally on the railway, his wife acting as the crossing keeper. For being available 24 hours a day, 7 days a week, she would be paid just a few pounds.

The nature of the job meant she could never leave the house, but in order to allow her to do a weekly shop, she was allowed every Friday afternoon off, between 2pm and 6pm. During these four hours, cover was provided by the early turn porter from Attenborough Station (6am - 2pm shift).

This meant that every third week on a Friday afternoon, I would start work at 6am, leave the Station at about 1.50pm and cycle to Barton Lane. A small wooden hut was provided for when temporary crossing keepers were in attendance. This was situated south of the railway, on the opposite side of the road to the cottage. It was about eight feet square, and inside was an old armchair, a solid fuel stove and supply of coal, and a kettle to boil water. A pitcher of water would be provided by the crossing keeper. Also installed were two 'indicators', one for the up and one for the down line. These were glass-faced dials, about 6 inches diameter, being linked to the nearby signal boxes. Each had a needle, which indicated 'line clear' or 'line blocked'. Provided both showed 'line clear' that meant no trains were approaching and it was safe to open the gates. 'Line blocked' meant a train was approaching and gates could not be opened.

Each gate was a heavy, wooden, five-barred style gate and was always kept locked by a padlock. The procedure was simple. When a vehicle arrived, as soon as both lines were clear, the gate opposite the side where the vehicle was would be unlocked and opened, then the other gate. This was to prevent the driver encroaching onto the line whilst the other gate was being opened. In the rare event of two vehicles approaching from opposite directions at the same time, the drivers were instructed not to start crossing until both gates were open.

The level of traffic varied. I can remember some days when not a single vehicle came down the lane all afternoon. On other occasions, such as when there as a fishing match on the Trent, one barely had time for a sit down and cup of tea all afternoon! (A.Dance August 2012)

Barton Lane, linking Nottingham, Chilwell Retail Park, Village hotel and the Sewage works, is currently the main access road to Attenborough Nature Reserve and its eco-friendly award winning Visitor Centre which was opened by Sir David Attenborough in 2005. In an effort to reduce carbon emissions, this building uses electricity generated from heat pumps set below the water. Not only has the landscape

Barton Lane

dramatically changed in the last hundred years but the ownership and allegiance too. Once firmly in the grasp of the Warrens of Toton Manor, the name declares its postal and parish address as Attenborough.

The gravel workings, (Trent Gravels Ltd) begun in 1929, have completely changed the once productive fields and meadows forever. The Nature Reserve occupies a series of lagoons and islands within the flooded gravel workings. These offer rich habitats for a great variety of birds and other wildlife. Winter wildfowl, including the shy bittern visit here as do many migratory birds, many of which breed on the islands which are carefully managed by Nottinghamshire Wildlife Trust. Resident bird populations enjoy the habitats and in 2012 the heronry here recorded a very large population of this elegant bird. People also flock to this area for the

Attenborough Nature Reserve Visitor centre opened 2005

peace and beauty. Fishing, photography, ornithology and walking are popular pursuits which are enjoyed here.

Barton Lane, Coneries Farm, Barton Ferry & Farm

Barton Lane leads to Barton Ferry, passing such houses as 'The Warren' and 'The Retreat' and enabling farmers from the Coneries or Ferry Farm to have access to the River Trent and Barton in Fabis.

The Warren, at the start of it's life, 1920s

The two wooden bungalows called 'The Warren' and 'The Retreat' were built soon after the First World War. Thomas Gillman, then farmer of the Coneries Farm, bought the buildings from the military encampment at Clifton and used the wood to build the bungalows. He then sold Coneries Farm, except for twelve acres and moved into 'The Warren'. Sadly he and his wife died shortly afterwards, but his daughter and new husband stayed there and raised a family. A former resident recalls, "It *was like being on holiday all the time. We (twin sisters) had pets galore and walked across stiles and meadows to Attenborough Preparatory School. When we were older, we cycled to the main road, and caught the bus to school. It was lovely then, lots of birds and flowers. 'The Warren, is now under water.*"

Another occupant of the area was Mr Sutton who rented a few fields and ran a small holding. He kept a couple of cows, a horse and a few pigs.

Whilst the area was trouble free and idyllic, there was one tragic event. A suicide and murder was discovered along Barton Lane. resulting from a suicide pact. A rumour circulated that these lovers could never be together as one partner was already married. The trauma was caused to the people finding their bodies.

River Erewash and water meadows

To reach these bungalows or the farms, one had to cross the railway. It was a gated crossing which was operated by Mr and Mrs Spurr (1930s). There was a bell hanging by the gate to ring or if one was in a car, the car horn could be used. *The lady (Mrs Spurr) slowly answered the hoot, "'as yer been 'ooting?"*

There was also an unmanned crossing from the farm, where the occasional accident occurred. A farm worker had a lucky escape in 1962, when the 10.41 diesel train from Nottingham to Derby loomed up in dense fog, cutting the tractor in two. The front passenger coach was derailed, but no-one was hurt.

Coneries Farm

Coneries farm was situated off a track from Barton Lane. It was a typical farm, with a tall farmhouse and barns situated around a farmyard. The house, larger than Toton Manor House, was built sometime around 1800, a sign of wealth and standing. It is described in 1804 as a *"Modern built dwelling house, containing a hall, two parlours, kitchen, and eight good lodging*

Coneries farmhouse, barns and remnants of ornamental garden

rooms." The house was for sale in that year along with *"..two barns, stabling for twelve horses, a coach house, a convienent farm yard and a garden walled to the north and east well planted with fruit trees."*[1] Sixty years later Conery House estate came up for sale again and improvements were seen to have been carried out. Internal plumbing had arrived with the inclusion of a toilet or water closet.

It was during the early 19th century that a Mr John Jowett Glover of Potlock House, Findern, near Derby, farmed here. Following his death and the death of his wife in the Coneries some years later, an auction sale listed "superior live and dead animals" so one can suppose that Mr Jowett Glover built this second property to raise his prize animal stock on the rich and nutritious water meadows. The farming stock consisted mainly of sheep, with a few cows, eight horses, pigs, chickens and three pairs of ducks. There were many farm implements included in the auction, such as turnip pulper, superior winnowing machine, an iron scuffler, three sets of harrows and two iron ploughs.

THE CONERIES.

Reps. of late Thomas Morris	189	House, Outbuildings, Yard, Garden, Orchard, Plantations, &c.							1	2	19
	190	Little Hill Close					Old Turf		2	1	15
	191	Bottom Orchard					Old Turf		0	1	31
	192	The Meadow					Old Turf		7	2	15
	193	House Close					Old Turf		11	3	35
	194	Osiers					Old Turf		1	0	37
	195	The Bottoms					Old Turf		5	1	39
	196	Askew Nook					Old Turf		3	2	17
	197	Great Hill Close					Arable		7	2	29
	198	Stack Yard Close					Arable		8	1	14
	199	Long Close					Arable		10	3	6
	200	Handkerchief Close					Arable		4	0	24
	201	Brick Kiln Close					Arable		9	2	1
	202	The Flat Close					Arable		10	0	21
	203	Toton Close					Arable		12	0	0
	204	Osiers					Osiers or Wood		0	0	25
	205	Osiers					Osiers or Wood		0	2	9
	206	Little Robin Holme (In Long Eaton)				Old Turf		2	0	3
	207	Robin Holme (In Long Eaton)					Old Turf		12	0	14
	208	Osiers (In Long Eaton)					Grass		2	1	33
	209	Osiers (In Long Eaton)					Osiers		2	1	9
	186	Far Home Leys					Old Turf		5	0	30
	185	Home Leys					} Old Turf		13	3	5
	184	Far Little Inns									
	187	Attenborough Meadow					Old Turf		38	1	0
	188	Part of ditto					Old Turf		1	1	12
									175	0	1
						Carried forward			351	0	15

1892 sale Document Toton Estate

The field names give clues as to their shape, size or use. The fields on Coneries Farm, now mostly underwater, include Handkerchief Close, Brick Kiln Close, Stackyard Close, Askew Nook, The Flatt and Willow Holt. Willow was an important and saleable commodity especially during the 19th century, osiers used in basket making grew by the rivers and several willow holts, where willow was also grown are marked on the surveys of Toton Manor. These willows, once cut, would have been sold to the basket makers higher up the River Trent, near Newark and beyond.

---

[1] Derby Mercury May 17th 1804 advertisement feature

In the 20th century there were four people working on this 200 acre mixed farm: a housemaid, two cowmen and a housemaid. The live-in staff occupied the top floor of this three storey building. The floors were uneven. "*My dad used to work here as a horseman and ploughman and I remember crawling on the uneven floor studying the reeds and plaster.*" (This boy went

on to become a Wildlife Conservation Officer.) Crops such as wheat and oats for cattle food were important aspects of the farm's life. During the Second World War, German and Italian prisoners of war had to help on the farm. They also erected the corrugated fence which at one time bordered Barton Lane. They travelled daily from Wollaton Hall encampment.

Working in the orchard, circular saw

Ginger a Suffolk Punch

Ploughing was done by horse power. At one time there would have been about eighteen horses on the farm, of which about three pairs would be working horses such as Suffolks. "My dad was the horseman and ploughman for the Coneries." Cyril Lewis, the horseman, was fond of saying " *Give me a horse any day, you can't talk to a tractor.*"

A Dutch barn (a familair site in the Englsih countryside at one time) stood beside the farm storing the hay needed for the animals in winter.

The cattle were herded in for milking from where the sailing club is today. Milking, was another manual task, with the milk stored in churns. The Bennett family, ran the farm and a small dairy business, mostly supplying Long Eaton. A great achievement around 1950 was the purchase of a wonderful electric van, which made life a lot easier; no ponies to catch!

Bennett milk float

The farm gradually declined and bird watching grew. Coneries Farm with its varied birdlife became a popular place to ring birds in order to study their migrations. "*It must be sad to think lads of our generation played in the derelict rooms of this lovely, sturdy old house. Later, as bird ringers, we used the downstairs rooms as 'ringing labs' as we caught birds in the fields around and took them indoors to weigh and measure them. On cold winter days in 1969 to 1973 we could guarantee catching many farmland finches with nets set up along the derelict hedgerows because some of the fields were still cultivated with spring cereals before quarrying went through the area. I have only ever caught one little owl and that was in a net set up along the fence in front of the house in Feb 1969."* (S Aitken)

The farm itself, the land where an old Romany caravan stood and the bridge over the River Erewash have all been swallowed up by Trent Gravels (now Cemex) and incorporated into Attenborough Nature Reserve. The name 'Conery' reflects the past association with rabbits or coneys. A near by cul-de-sac, Connery mews is possible named with reference to the old farm or possibly, though, to Sean Connery.

Bird Ringing Group & students utilise the old Coneries Farm buildings

Bennett family party, by stylish front porch

Many fond memories of people and places still linger. Charles Bennett began the family tradition of farming, at The Limes smallholding, augmenting this small farm with rented fields eslewhere in Toton. He then took his family to Coneries Farm, a much bigger enterprise. His son, William Ellis Bennett, carried on and his son Peter, after him. An excerpt in the local Parish magazines records *"the death of Mr W.E. Bennett of the Coneries farm, Toton ...with his old time courtesy and courage, for Billy, as he was affectinonately known was always one of the kindliest of men."* (March 1947)

The other farm at the southern edge of Toton Manor estate was Ferry farm.

Ferry Farm alias Chamberlain's Farm alias Plowright's farm.

This two storey building, demolished

Chamberlains Farm c1954

in the late 20th century, replaced an older building possibly on the same site. The farmhouse stood a little way back from the river, undoubtedly because of the possibility of flooding. *"The old Barton Ferry House, long since demolished, stood on the west side of the River Erewash and was subject to frequent flooding. A Mr Woolley, who was a ferry man at Barton Ferry, used to tell how he always had to save his pigs and poultry by taking them upstairs whenever a flood occurred."*[2]

---

[2] Lysons Derbyshire 1817 Long Eaton and Sawley Archive

Ferry Farm was a small farm in the 1950s, with just three fields used for grazing and for hay. The farm buildings themselves were a little behind the house and were composed of a series of barns, one of which had accommodation for ten cows. These barns were later used for storage, including canoes owned by local residents.

The farmer combined his agricultural duties with those of a ferryman. It appears to have always been a small farm, as undoubtedly the combination of farmer and ferryman was

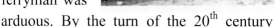
Farmyard of Ferry farm

arduous. By the turn of the 20th century when George Roadley was farmer and ferryman, the farm had grown to around 46 acres. George Roadley left the farm in 1910 to farm a larger farm in Leicestershire.[3]

Dennis Radford ,haymaking on Chamberlain's farm c 1950

The rights of ferry were guarded by the major landowner. The tenant does the work and the landowner takes the profit! Having being sold in the 17th century to the Sacheverell family, they are then found back in the records of Toton Manor some time later. In the Toton Manor book, it records *"Annexed to the farm is the fishing in the River Trent and a ferry across the said river leading to Barton also an island of about one acre and a half. The tenant agrees to plant the island at his own expense providing he pays no additional rent for the same for the next five years. The land is very fertile and the Spinney produces full as much profit is cut once in every three years and said to be generally sold for eight pounds the acre. In the fishery there are good salmon caught but not as much small fish. The ferry being not for carriages is said to produce profit over and above the repairs to the boats and which is done by the tenant."*[4]

The farm has had a succession of tenant farmers cum ferrymen over the centuries. The Ballard family lived and worked here for many years (maybe even over 200 years). In 1802 John Ballard renewed his lease of the orchards, messuages, tenements, outbuildings and appurtenances. He also leased the boats

extract of survey map 1846 showing position of Ferry farm

[3] Article in Nottinghamshire Historian Thomas Roadley The Flying Teacher.
[4] 1788 John Ballard's farm Toton Manor Book

and the fishing rights as well as several plots of meadow ad pasture land, namely Osier Bed, Home Leys, and Nook Piece, totalling just over eleven acres.

Barton Ferry

This ancient ferry, a source of income for the Lords of Toton Manor, served a useful service to farmers, travellers or 20th century pleasure seekers. Many people used to cross to Barton in Fabis

Barton Ferry, early 1900s.

to enjoy a drink in the tea rooms, or go for a walk in the woods, pick bluebells and other wildflowers or just enjoy a ramble or a picnic in the area. The ferry was used as an access to the leafy lanes of Clifton and the tea room at Barton in Fabis. In an early 20th century book of rambles in Nottinghamshire the author writes about the section from Barton in Fabis *"The meadow path is approached and very soon the slow laboorius splash of dipping oars falls as soothing music around and we pass south to north across the silvery Trent to take the homeward trail."* Another writer also describing routes for rambles remarks *"...we come to the banks of the Trent where a ferry has been standing from time immemorial. Indeed it is considered to have formerly been one of the greatest thoroughfares to the north."*

In the 1930s on a sunny afternoon it was common to see a queue and sometimes this queue was 200 or more people waiting to cross. Sunday school outings and later Scout and Guide outings also utilised this service. Dorothy Tatman Superintendent of Toton Sunday School, reported one such enjoyable occasion in 1948.

Toton Notes.

We have introduced a Youth Club for Sunday School Scholars, thus they are learning to worship, work and play to together.

On Good Friday the children attended the Morning Service at Attenborough. In the afternoon, escorted by Miss Walters, Mr. Haddon, and myself, they enjoyed a ferry-ride across the river and a walk to Gotham, where they had tea, played games, and enjoyed the early spring sunshine. On Easter Day, Teachers escorted the the children to Attenborough for the Children's Service.

This ferry itself was a small, flat-bottomed rowing boat "not suitable for carriages", operated for many years. It had space for twenty people. The cost of a journey cost one penny or one and half pence with a bike. The farmer Mr Plowright of Barton in Fabis used to take his prize Shire horses across by boat to the rich meadows on the Toton side each summmer. The ferry also used occasionally to transport cattle but the preferred way was to take the cattle to Weir Field, Beeston, and cross when the water was low in the summer. There were two boats at Barton: the large 20 seater and a small one which could be rowed single handed. Horace Johnson rowed every day in this small boat to Barton in Fabis, where he left the boat by the bank and went off to work. The boat was therefore waiting for him to return

Barton ferry in action

home in the evenings.

The boat propelled by long oars (over 7 feet long), was operated by the Chamberlain family for many years. George Chamberlain was followed by his son Arthur.

Various 'helpers' on Sunday afternoons earned themselves a bit of pocket money. Alf

Barton ferry 1950s.

Barton remembers earning enough pocket money, by helping operate the boat, to enable him to buy a bike.

Beside the ferry was a hut accessed by three steps. Here prospective passengers could wait in inclement weather. It was also that some locals played cards and here that the young people of the area began to congregate here on many a summer evening (no discos, night clubs or other entertainment then.)

The ferry was a source of income but also expense. The upkeep of the boats in 1788 was said to equal the money received for crossings. A succession of ferrymen have operated here, navigating the tricky waters. The current of the River Trent is quite strong, especially when in flood. This affects the boats as they have to be rowed in a curve or arc rather than just straight across. The technique is to row into the centre of the river upstream and then drift into the Barton in Fabis bank, using the current.

Accidents, though, have happened in the past. One such event in 1545 is recorded in the

Painting by P. Barsby c 1920s Ferry hut and River Trent

Calendar of Inquests. *On 20th February 1545 when Richard Coll, William Pyggyn, Robert Sleigh and Joan Thurman intended to cross the River Trent in a small boat called Barton*

Boote (boat) in which there were three mares while they were steering with a rope (mares tied with a rope to the boat?) the rope suddenly broke and the boat was overturned by the force of the flow of the river and all four of them were drowned.

Ferrymen, such as the Chamberlains had to be called to operate the boats. A bell hanging by the farm gate or a shout "Oi Ferry" aroused the attention of the ferryman in good or bad weather. *"From the farmhouse... a raincoated becapped figure emerges to tramp with a firm step to the moored ferry boat. Not a young figure, obviously, but a strong one it is George Chamberlain, rising ninety who still continues the long line of ferrymen that go back to Saxon and probably early British times. His strong biceps and back muscles still give a daily service under his contract which refers to the "ancient ferry" formerly owned by Mr T.I.Birkin and later Mr T.H.Barton."*. The newspaper article in 1949 evokes a picture of hardwork and service.

George Chamberlain - flat cap and moustache 1949

Horses, such as the Shire horses, belonging to Mr Plowright, swam across the Trent attached to the ferry boat with a rope. One unfortunate horse, crossing from the Ferry house side was not so lucky. A young lady and her horse wishing to cross (circa 1950), approached the ferry. The horse refused to go into the water and so Arthur Chamberlain believing all horses could swim, blindfolded the horse and led it into the river, whereupon it went straight down.

Arthur Chamberlain was the last ferryman, and is remembered for his flat cap worn at a jaunty angle, who rode his bike with legs akimbo and his heels on his pedals. He had a genial manner with a quiet smiling face and was always on the lookout for a bargain. He augmented his farmer and ferryman duties with renting out the caravans parked in the orchard. After he left the farm he became the Vermin Operative at Chilwell Depot (the rat catcher).

Nudd's boat on the River Trent

Close to the ferry, Mr Nudd's boat was moored for many years, close to his house built on stilts. Also close to Barton Ferry various ancient items have been discovered. Two mammoth teeth were found:...*two large mammoth teeth which were found in Toton parish, near to Barton Ferry, in the Trent gravel, five feet deep; one is the right molar tooth, about 12 inches by 7 inches. (R. Mellors)* Ancient axes have also been found in the gravels, showing the long history of Toton area.

Local Sport – Football Rex Wyatt

The activity in sport, in Toton, is greater than ever before. Cricket, tennis, bowls and football all take place in the locality. Manor Farm Recreation Ground is particularly busy with various football teams.

John Northfield (or is it Tommy Lawton?) -Manor Park

Toton F.C[1] Juniors and Toton Tigers have many teams, covering a wide age range. Senior teams also use the two pitches between the rivers. Before the footbridge was erected there was only one pitch with changing facilities in one old railway wagon. The first teams playing in Toton were the Soldiers and Sailors' Club, who played behind The Limes where the houses on Doris, Shirley and Angela Courts now stand.

Toton Old Boys team 1953 - Archie Walters in the flat cap

Toton Old Boys, that is the senior team, played regularly. Members of the team included Roy Key, Maurice Ogley, Eric Brailsford, Norman Hallam and Cyril Allsop. Toton Youth Club was another club that played in the 1950s.

Toton United, established in the early 1960s, was probably the most successful team to play on the park. Terry Pickering (centre forward) and Brian Smith were brilliant centre forwards with Terry Pickering definitely the highest goal

Cup winners

scorer. In one game alone he scored 8 out of 9 goals in a 9-2 victory against Burnham Products, ably assisted by Stuart Mitchell. This was a Notts. Junior Cup game, on our way to the semi-finals. We actually beat Everton[2] in an early round. Also 'Centre Halfs' never came better than Dave Frost, Martin Northfield or Charney.

Toton United 1963 Terry Pickering with the ball

[1] FC Football Club
[2] Everton is a small village near Bawtry Notts

A Professional Footballer - Frank Austin

To my knowledge, the only professional sports person to be brought up in Toton, was Frank Austin. Born in Stoke-On-Trent, in 1933, he moved to Carrfield Avenue, Toton and attended the local school from 1939 to1944, before moving to Grange School which at that time was the nearest Secondary School, when he was eleven. He became Captain of the Long Eaton and District Boys' team. He played on grounds like Chesterfield and Grimsby at the age of fourteen. He was then selected to play in the England Boys team versus Eire, an International game held at Britten Park, Brentfield, on May 8th 1948.

After leaving school, he played for Toton F.C. and it was from there that Coventry City club signed him in 1950. He played in 302 games, making his debut in 1953 against Newport County. In 1963 Jimmy Hill took over as manager and Frank's face didn't fit. He made a move to Torquay United for a small fee, making twenty four league appearances, then Chelmsford City in March 1964, making fifty appearances, then Brentford in 1965, before retiring and moving back to Long Eaton in 1967.

Walter Winterbottom, the England manager, came to watch him for possible selection for England. He unfortunately got injured and had to be carried off. Sadly Frank passed away in July 2004 aged 71 years.

Frank Austin at Coventry City wearing no 3 shirt

" ...Austin represented England as a schoolboy and was a stylish and composed performer... His lack of height hampered him at wing-half and he was successfully converted into a full-back in 1956. He made his most appearances in a season in 1959-60 when he played 43 games – 41 in the league as City went close to promotion from Division Three." Extract from Obituary 2004

Toton Bowling Maureen Gunn

The bowling green at Manor Farm was laid in the 1960s and in 1982 it became the home of Manor Bowls Club. The newly formed club consisted of twenty-eight bowlers who had completed a six week course to learn the game and were keen to take it further.

Through friendly matches, the Club soon became accepted in the locals bowling season and it was not long before they became a force to be reckoned with in the various EBA and EBF[3] leagues. Thirty years on, only three of the founder

First Competitive game, Arnold Park 1983

members still play for the Club, but Manor remains the respected, caring club it has always been, and new members can be sure of a friendly welcome.

Other Sports

Tennis courts occupy a site facing Nottingham road. This facility is open to the general public.

Winners of Beeston League Cup 2009

Further along on the Recreation site is the cricket pitch, beyond which, close to the Greenwood Centre is a facility aimed at the modern generation who enjoy basketball in a less formal situation.

Sport is for all.

Toton Cricket Club c1960

---

[3] EBA – English Bowling Association, EBF English Bowling Federation

Conclusion

The landscape of Toton has changed forever. From flat meadows where once Ice Age animals roamed and Bronze Age men hunted and fished for food, the land has been shaped, by men, first for agriculture, then for industry and finally for residential purposes. Toton hamlet has become a dormitory town.

Fields where wheat, peas and barley grew and when horses and cows were the main source of power are no longer there, replaced by houses, roads, wires and cables. Gravel is extracted where sheep grazed. Pantechnicons roar where horses trotted. Houses stand where fields were cultivated. The river, so important for trade, is

Agriculture and Industry bordering Derbyshire and Stapleford Notts 2012

now enjoyed as a leisure feature for its beauty for sailing boats. Not only has the landscape changed but our language too. We have gained words such as megabyte (computers) and lost words like threaves (sheep).

Working for others

Our world is a constantly changing one, with variety, one that enables us to live in all manner of ways. Who would have it different?

People are the key: their ideas, their actions and their abilities have formed and changed Toton over the Millennia. Famous faces have visited, stopped here for while, but it is the people of Toton itself, who have made it, have developed it and are still breathing life into it.

Their memories are personal and vary according to interests and experiences. Many versions of events may be circulating and many opinions abound, in this quiet 'unknown' part of south west Nottinghamshire.

River Erewash 2012

Toton is unique.

Appendix 1 Examples from Rent Book of Toton -   Ref DD/39/4 &DD/39/5 (Notts Archives)

John Jaques father of George Jaques-   **The halfs year Rent for ye Manor of Toton**   1620

John Jaques for the Middle Rice	£5
John Jaques for the ?	£30
John Jaques for the Trent Close	£9
John Jaques for the fifty shillings Rice	£7
John Jaques for the near Eastfield	£5
John Jaques for the Pinfold Close	£6
Jane jaques and John Jaques for the new Swannest	£3
John Jaques for Smiths house and commons	£3
John Jaques for the forty shilling Rice	£12
Half years and the 3 Staynyard	

Sum   £81 10s

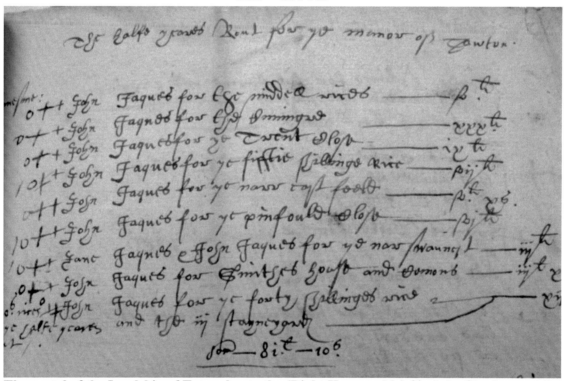

The rental of the Lordship of Toton due to the (Right Honourable) Sir John Stanhope at the feast of St Michael 1627

George Jaques for the Middle Rice	£5
For the ?	£30
Trent close	£9
The 50 shilling Rice	£7
The near Eastfield	£12
The Pinfold Close	£6
The Swannest Close	£3
The 40 shilling Rice	£12
The Smiths Close house and commons	£3

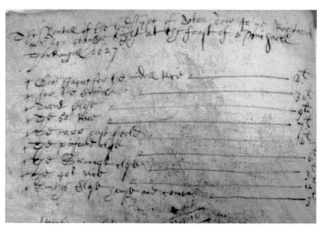

Appendix 2 Hearth Tax Records   (Thoroton & W.F. Webster Nottingham Central Library)

Toton   Chargeable   1664 Attenborough is not listed separately, the two hamlets are here together.

Occupier	Number of hearths	tax
John Jacques	5	10s
Thomas Coming	1	2s
John Black	1	2s
George B (hole)ker	1	2s
John Canner	1	2s
George Johnson	1	2s
Widow Ballard	1	2s
William Ballard	1	2s
Richard Bucher	1	2s
John Eddington	1	2s
Peter Shaw	1	2s
Richard Johnson	1	2s
?John Badinge	1	2s
...?...es	1	2s
....?...lley – (Smalley?)	1	2s

Not Chargeable 1664	
Thomas Walker	1
Robert Aslin	1
Mary Dodson	1
Francis Boote	1
Robert Cates	1
Richard Day	1

1674 Chargeable name and number of hearths only

Arthur Warin Esq	6
William Balalrd(Ballard)	2
John Blake	2
Robert Elliott	1
Widow Cripple	2
John Collington	2
Widow Johnson	2
John Goodwin	2
Kath Barker	1
John Smalley	1
George Barker	2
Thomas Barker	1
Richard Singlehurst	1
George Constable	1
Thomas Deay (Day?)	1
Edward Bealy	1
Henry Deay (Day?)	1
William Wood (empty)	1

The number of hearths reflected the wealth and status of the occupier, with one hearth as "labourer, and the poorest sort of husbandmen". Two or three hearths were tradesmen or yeoman whilst four to seven hearths were merchants. The highest group, "gentility and noblemen" was not present in Toton. Their houses had eight or more hearths.

Appendix 3   1846 Toton Tithe Book ref. Extract PR8205

Landowner – Warren The Late Sir John Borlas(e) Bart; Trustee V(iscount) Francis Hurt esq and Others

Part of the land rented by John Earp, the numbers refer to the fields on the survey map AT 138b. This small book records the acreage and tithes paid to Vicar and also to Impropriator –

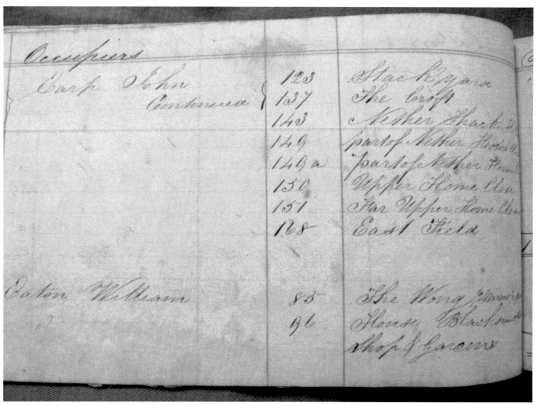

Chesterfield School- the Charity of Foljambe

In total John Earp rented 187 acres 2 rods 27 perches. He paid the vicar £11 15s and 8d. He paid the Impropriator £10 18s and 7d. He paid the Trustees of Sir John Borlas(e) Warren (a twice yearly rent, not shown in this document)

William Eaton rented 5 acres 1 pole and 4 perches. He paid the vicar 16s 3d and the Impropriator 5 shillings.

Appendix 4

Grange Farm
Restaurant

TOTON NOTTINGHAM
LONG EATON 69426

Dinner £5.75 inc. of VAT & Service

Smoked Salmon 85p extra
Prawn Cocktail 45p extra
Fillet of Smoked Mackerel with Coleslaw & Horseradish Sauce   Avocado Pear with Prawns
Fresh Grapefruit Polynesian Style   Canneloni in Tomato Sauce   Country Style Pate
Battered Mushrooms with Sweet & Sour Sauce   Fresh Honeydew Melon with Ginger & Sugar
Fried Whitebait with Tartare Sauce   Poached Egg Florentine   Iced Tomato Juice
Hors d'Oeuvres

****

Fried Goujons of Plaice with Tartare Sauce   Orange & Pineapple Sorbet   Seafood Pancake
Home Made Cream of Chicken & Mushroom or French Onion Soup

****

Poached Salmon with Shrimp Sauce
Grilled Rainbow Trout with Almonds
Whole Lemon Sole Tropicale
Supreme of Chicken flamed in Brandy & thickened with Mushrooms & Cream
Fillet of Beef Strogonoff
Sauted Lambs Kidneys in Port & thickened with Cream
Braised Steak Pieces in Burgundy Sauce
Roast Best End of English Lamb with Redcurrant Jelly
Roast Loin of Pork with Gooseberry Sauce & Stuffing
Grilled Minute Steak Chasseur
Escalope of Veal Holstein
Farm-House Grill 30p extra
Roast Aylesbury Duckling with Blackcurrants 50p extra
Grilled Entrecote Steak with Onions & Mushrooms 65p extra
Garden Peas
Broccoli Spears in Clear Butter
New & Parmentier Potatoes

****

Sherry Trifle   Profiteroles with Chocolate Sauce   Strawberry Ice Cream   Peach Melba
Apple Pie with Fresh Cream   Pineapple Cheesecake   Ice Cream with Creme de Cassis
Fresh Strawberries with Dairy Cream   Meringue Chantilly   Fresh Fruit Salad with Cream
Blackcurrant Meringue Pie   Bavarian Chocolate Gateau   Waknut Sundae   Banana Split
utter Almond Ice Cream   Green Figs with Cream   Caramel Meringue Glace   Creme Caramel
Pears Belle Helene

****

Selection of Cheese, Butter & Biscuits

****

Coffee with Cream

Appendix 5   Coronation Events 1953

Toton Ward.

★

PROGRAMME OF EVENTS

★

May 11.   Coronation Tea to be given by members of Toton Social Services' Club, at Grange Farm, for the Old People of Toton.

May 31.   A Drumhead Service will be held on the Toton Primary
3 p.m.   School Field, taken by a Padre of Chilwell Ordnance Depot.

June 1.   An exhibition of Arts and Crafts at Toton Primary
2-8 p.m.   Schools. Entries open to Toton Residents. Certificates will be awarded according to group: Leatherwork, Painting, Metalwork, Raffiawork, Woodwork, Knitting, etc., Embroidery, etc., Feltwork.

June 2.   A Camp Fire will be lit on Portland Road Recreation
7.30 p.m.   Ground arranged by the Scouts and Girl Guide Associations of Chilwell. Join them in their sing song. Refreshments will be provided.

June 3.   The exhibition of Arts and Crafts will again be open
2-8 p.m.   at the Toton Primary Schoolroom.

June 4.   A Talent Competition will be held in Toton Primary
7.15 p.m.   Schoolroom open to all people in Toton. Entries will be judged in the following sections: Instrumental, Vocal, Elocution, Dancing. Prizes will be awarded to each group.

June 6.   A Fancy Dress Parade open to all ages and people in
12.30 p.m.   Toton. Assemble on the Recreation Ground on Portland Road at 12.30 p.m. and walk round the village.

1.45 p.m.   Sports. For children of 15 years of age and under to take place on the Toton Primary School Field. A Coronation Tea will be given to all children attending the Sports. The prizes won by the different events taking place during the week, also winners of the different sports, will be presented after the close of the Sports. An Open-Air Dance will be held on the Toton Primary Schoolyard after the presentation of prizes.

June: 7.   A Service will be held on the Toton Primary School
11 a.m.   Field, taken by a Clergyman.

Prizes will be presented to the three best decorated houses in the village of Toton.

Certificates will be awarded to the householders of the best dressed street or part thereof.

Notices and Entry Forms will be available at a later date.

Appendix 6 — Butterflies, Birds, Plants of Toton Fields Nature Reserve (2012)

Butterflies	Birds		Plants – Trees /Plants
Toton Hill	Mute swan	Fairly common visitor	Alder
Small Skipper	Pink –footed Goose	Occasionally flying over	Ash
Essex Skipper	Greylag Goose	Occasionally flying over	Silver Birch
Large Skipper	Canada Goose	Often flying over	Blackthorn
Clouded Yellow	Eurasian Teal	Uncommon winter visitor	Wild Cherry
Brimstone	Mallard	Fairly common resident	Hawthorn
Large White	Tufted Duck	Uncommon winter visitor	Holly
Small White	Goosander	Uncommon winter visitor	Black Poplar
Green veined White	Red –legged Partridge	Uncommon resident	Black Bryony
Orange Tip	Grey Partridge	Uncommon resident	Black Medick
Small Copper	Common Pheasant	Uncommon resident	Hedge Bedstraw
Brown Argus	Great Crested Grebe	Uncommon visitor	Bluebell
Common Blue	Cormorant	Fairly common visitor	Bramble
Holly Blue	Little Egret	Uncommon visitor	Bristly Ox-Tongue
Red Admiral	Grey Heron	Common visitor	Broom
Painted Lady	Sparrowhawk	Fairly common resident	Buttercup
Small Tortoiseshell	Buzzard	Fairly common visitor	Campion
Peacock	Kestrel	Uncommon resident	Cat's Ear
Comma	Moorhen	Common resident	Centuary
Speckled Wood	Coot	Uncommon visitor	Common Bent Grass
Marbled White	Stock Dove	Common resident	Cocks Foot Grass
Wall	Wood Pigeon	Common resident	Tufted Hair Grass
Gatekeeper	Collared Dove	Common resident	Cow Parsely
Meadow Brown	Cuckoo	Uncommon visitor	Cransebill
Ringlet	Barn Owl	Rare	Dead-nettle
Small Heath	Green Woodpecker	Resident	Evening Primrose
Toton Sidings	Great Spotted Woodpecker	Resident	Goat's Rue
Small Skipper	Skylark	Uncommon resident	Good King Henry
Dingy Skipper	Pied Wagtail	Uncommon resident	Clover
Large White	Wren	Common resident	Hawkbit
Small White	Dunnock	Common resident	Bird's Foot Trefoil
Green veined White	Robin	Common resident	Hairy Bittercress
Orange Tip	Blackbird	Common resident	Marsh Marigold
Small Copper	Fieldfare	Common winter visitor	Marsh Thistle
Brown Argus	Song Thrush	Fairly common resident	Melilot
Common Blue	Redwing	Common winter visitor	Bee Orchid
Small Tortoiseshell	Mistle Thrush	Fairly common resident	Pineapple Weed
Peacock	Blackcap	Common summer visitor	Ox Eye Daisy
Speckled Wood	Lesser Whitethroat	Uncommon summer visitor	Poppy
Gatekeeper	Common Whitethroat	Common summer visitor	Purple Loosetrife
Meadow brown	Chiff Chaff	Fairly common visitor	Reedmace
Ringlet	Willow Warbler	Common summer visitor	Scarlet Pimpernel
Small Heath	Goldcrest	Uncommon resident	Self-heal
	Willow Tit	Fairly common resident	Speedwell
	Long -tailed Tit	Common resident	Teasel
	Coal Tit	Common resident	Toadflax
	Blue Tit	Common resident	Vetch
	Great Tit	Common resident	Wall Barley
	Magpie	Common resident	Wild Carrot
	House Sparrow	Common resident	Wild Angelica
	Tree Sparrow	Uncommon resident	Willow – Goat
	Carrion Crow	Common resident	Willow – Osier
	Linnet	Common resident	Willow – Crack
Brian Parkes	**Ainslie Carruthers** 53 out of 103 species listed		*Ainslie Carruthers* A selection from a long list

Appendix 7

Extract -Sale of Conery House estate Advertised in Derby Mercury September 13th 1865

BY MESSRS. NEWBOLD & OLIVER.

NOTTINGHAMSHIRE AND DERBYSHIRE.
VALUABLE FREEHOLD RESIDENTIAL ESTATE.

TO BE SOLD BY AUCTION,
BY MESSRS. NEWBOLD AND OLIVER,

At the MIDLAND HOTEL, in Derby, on MONDAY, the 16th day of October, 1865, at Three o'clock in the Afternoon, subject to such conditions as will be then produced;

THE CONERY HOUSE ESTATE, situated chiefly in the Township of Toton, in the County of Nottingham, the remainder thereof being in the Township of Long Eaton, in the County of Derby, and containing 118A. 1R. 22P. or thereabouts.

The whole of the Estate is land-tax redeemed. The lands in Toton are subject to a chief rent of 2s. per annum. The House contains dining, drawing, and breakfast rooms, kitchens, bakehouse, larder, pantry, dairy, three principal bed-rooms, four attics, water closet, store closets, and excellent cellaring. It is very conveniently arranged for being added to, at a comparatively small expense, to any extent that a purchaser might desire.

It has a southern aspect, looking upon an ornamental Lawn, with Ha-ha Fence, and it commands extensive and picturesque views of the neighbouring country, including the beautiful woods of Barton and of Thrumpton, and the celebrated Clifton Grove.

The outbuildings are extensive, including stabling, carriage-house, cow-sheds, piggeries, barn, granaries, and all other conveniences necessary for the profitable occupation of the land, and the yards are spacious and well adapted.

The Estate is very compact. It is bounded to a considerable extent by the beautiful river Erewash, a capital fishing stream, which runs through a portion of the property. It is also bounded in part by the navigable River Trent, and by lands of Sir Arthur Clifton and William Birkin, Esq. The land is of very superior quality, and is noted for the excellent state of its cultivation and its abundant crops. It is well timbered, having several very thriving plantations with plenty of cover for game, of which there is a good stock. The Orchards and Gardens are well stocked with choice fruit trees in full bearing.

The Derby and Nottingham Line of the Midland Railway intersects the Estate, and there are abundant facilities for transit, the distance from the Attenborough Station being about half-a-mile, from the Long Eaton Station about a mile, and from the great Central Station, "the Trent," a little over two miles. By road the Estate is situated seven miles from Nottingham and ten from Derby. The Quorn hounds and Mr. Musters' hounds meet in the immediate neighbourhood.

The Estate is brought into the market in consequence of the death of the late owner, Mrs. Glover, and as the lands are all in hand early possession may be had.

This Estate is peculiarly adapted to a gentleman of fortune wishing to make an establishment in the country, to form a small park with home farm. It offers all the requisities—shooting, fishing, proximity to hounds, picturesque situation, convenience to railways, first-class alluvial land, &c.

103

Sources

Newspapers

Neighbourhood News
Derby Mercury Newspaper online
Beeston Express
Beeston Gazette & Echo
Sandiacre & Stapleford News
Long Eaton Advertiser

Internet sources & Books

Long Eaton & Sawley Archive *www.archive.long-eaton.com*
Domesday Book- online
Then and Now -Nottinghamshire History
Attenborough Chilwell and Toton)
Census returns 1841 to 1911
Toton Yards and the Erewash Valley by David
Copeland
British Railways magazine Vol 1 no 3 Toton's
Yards
Memories of Working at Toton Sidings and beyond
by Bill Roys
A basketful – Rodney Cousins
St Peter's Church Toton – 50 years of Worship
Chilwell 1939-45
Nottinghamshire Countryside magazine 1948
J.Bramley

Oral Discussions

Mrs E. Hall, Miss K Harrison, Mr A.S Taylor,
Mr N.Lewis, Mr S.Leighton, Mr & Mrs Litchfield,
Mr D Bateman, Mr & Mrs A. Weatherspoon,
Miss H Knewstubb, Mr A Brand, Mr S Wilkinson,
Mrs Foster, Mrs S Wilkinson (nee Rooke),
Mrs J Norman (Davison), Mrs Gunn, Mr J Wright,
Mr W Whyatt, Mr P Bradley, Mr D. Radford,
 Mr & Mrs M Hammond, Mr & Mrs Tigg,
Mrs J Stewart (Mason) Mrs Austin, Mrs Costello,
Mr J Northfield, Mrs M Elliott, Mr A Culverwell

Held at Nottinghamshire Archives

Compounding Committee book vol iv p 2750
Toton Manor Rent Books 1620 – 1645 DD39/4- 6
 Rent books 1660 -1671DD39/7
Acreage of Toton before Enclosure
Survey of Toton DD WN 54-7
Parish meeting minutes1894-1934 PAC/80/1/1
Marriage settlement Mary Edge to John Jaques
DD/E/15/1
Register of teachers CC/Ed/SD/6/21
Court Book Toton Manor DD/39/1
Lady Warren Terrier DD/WN/58

Diversion of road 1920 DD 546/2
Toton Tithe Book PR 8205
Toton 1805 DD/WN/55
Meeting in Toton Chapel PR8191
Kersley Diary DD/1517/45
Toton 1845 AT 138/A, B, C
Plan Toton Manor TT3S
Indenture Bankruptcy Boler of Newark, maltster
r/e J Carter DD/H/180/67
Lease Barton Ferry, Fishery DD/WN/67/8
Farms, land Toton plan DD546/9
Land tax assessments for Toton 1940-1941
SO/IN/7/211
A plan of the Manor of Toton 1788 TT 3S
Off Licence PS/B/30/18
Licence for Off Licence C/PS/B/17/4
Toton Sale 1921 DD546/9
Kelly's, White's & Morris & Co Directories

Chester Archives

DVE 4/11 Vernon Collection

National Archives Kew

Chancery Rolls C54/15350 Indenture between
Vernon and Sherwin 1859

Nottingham Central Library-Local Studies Collection

Electoral Rolls
Nottingham Guardian newspaper
Transactions Thoroton Society Vol V
Thoroton record series Vol XVll Inquisitions
Thoroton record series Vol XXV Calendar of
Nottinghamshire Coroner's Inquests 1485-1558
edited by R.F.Hunisett
Barker's Walks around Nottingham

Beeston Library

Maps

Long Eaton Library

Long Eaton Co-operative Society a centenary
history 1868-1968

Beeston History Society

Chilwell 1939-1945 (history of life during Second
World War at Chilwell Ordnance Depot)
Beeston & Stapleford Official Guides and Street
Directory
Gregory's Rose catalogue 1969-Spring1970
Beeston & Stapleford U.D.C. Coronation
Festivities

Chetwynd Road Primary School

Log Books, Admission Books

Bispham Drive Junior School - Log Books

Photographs			
Page	*Photographs marked GM taken by the author Gillian Morral & RW Rex Wyatt*		
4	Aerial view Toton courtesy M.O.D. Chilwell Station	36	Stables courtesy J Davison
8	Aerial view Toton north unknown	36	Rear of The Limes 2012 GM
8	Aerial view Toton centre 1987 courtesy S.Leighton	37	Saddle room and office St Leonards courtesy J. Davison
9	Manor of Toton DD/WN/54 Nottinghamshire Archives GM	38	Gable end Patchitt's, Evesham Court GM
11	Court Book Toton Manor Nottinghamshire Archives DD/39/1 G.M	39	Gymkhana courtesy 1954 S Wilkinson
12	Extract Rent Book DD/39/6 Nottinghamshire Archives GM	38	Moor House 2012 GM
13	Extract from Map of Toton 1789 DD 39/11 (TT15) Nottinghamshire Archives GM	39	Kensington Close GM
14	Toton South Junction c 1935 unknown	39	Newsagent, Stapleford Lane, 2010 G M
14	River Erewash and bridge 2001 R Wyatt	40	Toton Endowed School group 1924 courtesy S.Wilkinson
15	Meandering By Pass Channel 2012 GM	41	Interior Toton Endowed School courtesy St Peter's
15	Willow viminalis, osiers 2012 GM	42	St Peter's Church1954 courtesy St Peter's
16	Garage courtesy B&DLHS	43	Interior St Peter's Church courtesy St Peter's
17	Garage (Burnett's) c1950 courtesy S. Burnett	43	St Peter's Church Interior – courtesy St Peter's
17	Garage circa 2001 RW	43	Pram Service courtesy St Peter's
17	Garage crane section NCCS003289 Courtesy of Reg Baker and www.picturethepast.org.uk	43 44	St Peter's exterior GM
18	Stan Burnett courtesy Mrs Burnett	44	Extract map Nottinghamshire Archives GM
18	House behind Manor Garage courtesy J.Gorin	44	Farmhouse, Whyatt's Farm courtesy E.Hall
18	Mill Farm mid 19th century courtesy K.Wilson	44	Barn, Whyatt's Farm courtesy E.Hall
19	Mill Farm sale notice courtesy P.Hammond	45	Rutland Ave, 2012 GM
19	Mr and Mrs Roberts c1900 courtesy K.Wilson	45	Marching out of C.O.D. courtesy M.O.D. Chilwell Station
20	Site plan Mill Farm DD/546/9 GM	46	Miss Blackshaw & class courtesy St Peter's
20	Toilet at Toton Corner RW	46	Old School Buildings courtesy Chetwynd Rd Primary Sch.
20	Police House High Rd RW	47	Toton School group Miss Day courtesy St Peter's Church
20	P.C.Stopp courtesy Mrs Stopp	47	Toton School Mrs Henson & class courtesy A.S Taylor
21	Manor Farm courtesy N.Lewis	48	Football team courtesy Mrs M. Elliott
21	Gatepost Manor Farm RW	48	Sports Day 1952 courtesy Mrs I Martin
21	Manor Farm courtesy N. Lewis	48	CDs Anne Briggs GM
22	Manor House sale 1892 courtesy P. Hammond	49	Chetywnd Rd Primary School Infant block 2010 GM
23	Manor Park from Nottingham Rd c 2000 RW	49	Dressing up at Toton school C.C.Day courtesy St Peter's
24	Millenium Sculpture Manor Park GM	49	Chetwynd Road RW
24	Manor Hotel (NCCS002314) - Courtesy of Reg Baker and www.picturethepast.org.uk	49	Malthouse courtesy A. Lewis
24	Kosie Cafe staff c 1940 courtesy S. Wilkinson	50	Toton Post Office courtesy J Crocker
25	Kosie Cafe c1950 courtesy S. Wilkinson	51	Post Office/ Crockers shop RW
25	Manor Pub courtesy RW	51	Mr & Mrs Crocker unknown
27	Shops, houses Nottingham Rd 2012 GM	51	Mr Edwin Jacklin courtesy E.Hall
28	Extract map AT 138A/B GM	52	Bungalow Stapleford Lane, 2012 GM
28	Cottage Cattery 18th century cottage, High Road GM	53	Hunt's Nurseries courtesy N.Lewis
28	Catherine Clarke & family courtesy S. Wilkinson	53	Former Co-op Hill View Road RW
29	Shoe concealed in 73 High Rd G Morral 2012	54	Chambers Cardboard Works c 1920 courtesy A. Hunt
29	Clay pipes 71 High road GM	54	Chambers Factory c 1979 Mr & Mrs Platt
30	Sunnydene repaired and modernised 2012 GM	55	Aerial view Chambers, Stapleford lane courtesy S. Leighton
31	Grange Farm Restaurant – postcard B&DLHS	55	Chambers end of era RW
31	Grange Farm 1909 courtesy S.Wilkinson	55	New beginnings St George's houses GM
32	Grange Farm 1964 unknown	56	Laying Foundation Stone 1962 courtesy S.Leighton
33	Grange Farm ballroom Promotional Booklet unknown	56	Building Methodist Church courtesy S. Leighton
33	Grange Farm interior Promotional Bklet Restaurant	57	Methodist Church 2012 Stapleford Lane GM
33	Womens' Social Service club Courtesy S Wilkinson	57	Toton Library 1955 courtesy Toton Library
34	Grange Farm (NCCS003282) - Courtesy of Reg Baker and www.picturethepast.org.uk	57	Interior Toton Library courtesy Toton Library
34	Grange Farm demolition courtesy Mrs Foster	57	Art Deco Library door courtesy Toton Library
35	The Limes 2012 GM	58	Warehouses C.O.D. courtesy B& DLHS
35	The Limes and doves courtesy J. Davison	58	Co-op Superstore (NCCS002905) - Courtesy of Ian Brown, LRPS and www.picturethepast.org.uk

58	Tesco Superstore GM	78	Chilwell Viaduct 1989 courtesy B&DLHS
59	Tesco Petrol Station 2012 GM	79	Rose Cottage c1912 courtesy S.Wilkinson
59	Turkey Oak, Swiney Way junction RW	79	Rose Cottage 2012 GM
59	Keeper's Cottage courtesy B& DLHS	80	Lorry crash, Long Cottage courtesy S. Wilkinson
60	View to site of Hill Farm, Ordnance Depot RW	81	Long Cottage courtesy S. Wilkinson
61	Rose GM	80	Long Cottage 2012 GM
63	View south looking down Stapleford Lane GM	80	Home- made toys courtesy S. Wilkinson
63	View from house, Darley Ave courtesy N. Lewis	81	Long Cottage c1900 courtesy S. Wilkinson
64	Ploughing Field Farm courtesy M. Costello	81	Chilwell Ordnance Depot courtesy private collection
64	Semi-detached house, courtesy M. Costello	83	Barton Lane level crossing & house 2012-GM
64	Spinney Woods unknown	84	Barton Lane courtesy N. Lewis
64	Banks Road site Spinney Wood R. Wyatt	84	Attenborough Nature Reserve Visitor C. courtesy B&DLHS
64	Frost's Garage Banks Road courtesy J. Wright	85	The Warren courtesy M. Antcliffe, J. Stewart nee Mason
65	Des Barnes & John Wight courtesy J. Wright	85	Water Meadows courtesy N. Lewis
65	Launch of Cavalier courtesy J. Wright	87	Coneries house & barns courtesy N. Lewis
65	Percy Sugden visits Frosts courtesy J. Wright	87	Coneries sale document courtesy P. Hammond
65	Green Goddess at Frosts courtesy J. Wright	87	Working Coneries orchard courtesy P. Mottram
66	Banks Road School 2010 GM	87	Ginger, a working horse courtesy P. Mottram
66	Outdoor area, Banks Road Infant School 2010 GM	87	Bennett's milk float courtesy P. Mottram
66	Bispham Drive Junior School courtesy Bispham Sch	88	Bird Ringing Coneries Farm courtesy N. Lewis
67	Opening ceremony courtesy Bispham Drive Jr School	88	Bennett family party courtesy P. Mottram
67	Visiting the library courtesy Bispham Drive Jr School	88	Chamberlain's Farm courtesy N. Lewis
67	Exterior Bispham Drive Junior School 2010 GM	89	Farmyard c1954 courtesy D. Bateman
68	Other Side of the Moon RW	89	Haymaking c1950 courtesy D.Radford
68	Chestnut Place, site of the pub, 2012 GM	89	Map extract Nottinghamshire Archives GM
68	Fish and Chip shop Woodstock Road 2012 GM	90	Barton ferry courtesy B&DLHS
68	Woodstock Rd Garage PP(NCCS002913) - Courtesy of Ian Brown, LRPS and www.picturethepast.org.uk	90	Barton Ferry courtesy B&DLHS
68	Terence Davies advert courtesy B&DLHS	91	Barton Ferry in action courtesy B&DLHS
70	Steam engine & trucks Fowler c 1959 RW	91	Barton Ferry boat early 1950s A Beniston
70	Control Tower North Receiving Sidings unknown	91	Hut by Barton Ferry from painting courtesy D. Bateman
70	Kitson shunting engine at Toton Sidings RW	92	George & Arthur Chamberlain, newspaper 1949
71	Grasses, wildflowers Toton Sidings Sept 2012 GM	92	Nudd's Boat courtesy private collection
71	Willowherb & Russian Vine Sept 2012 GM	93	Football, Manor Park courtesy Mr J Northfield
71	Bee on Spear Thistle Sept 2012 GM	93	Toton Old Boys unknown
71	Melilot, Toton Sidings 2012 GM	93	Cup Winners courtesy private collection
72	Greenwood Community Centre 2012 GM	93	Toton United courtesy Mr D Frost
72	Boys searching stream unknown	94	Frank Austin courtesy Mrs Austin
72	Carrfield Avenue 2012 GM	95	Competition 1983 courtesy Manor Bowls Club
73	House, Carrfield Avenue, 2012 GM	95	Winners League Cup courtesy Manor Bowls Club
73	80 Carrfield Rd as a shop courtesy K.Harrison	95	Toton Cricket Club courtesy Mrs M Elliott
73	Hairdressers, Carrfield Ave, 2012 GM	96	Agriculture & Industry 2012 GM
74	Birkin Ave, off Portland Rd courtesy B&DLHS	96	Working for others courtesy S. Leighton
74	Modern Housing Portland Road, 2012 GM	96	River Erewash 2012 GM
75	Mr Harrison & chrysanthemum courtesy K Harison	97	Extracts DD/39/4 Nottinghamshire Archives GM
75	Ceremony Coronation Hall, courtesy B&DLHS	97	Extracts DD/39/6 Nottinghamshire Archives GM
75	Work starts, Coronation Hall courtesy H. Knewstubb		
75	Work in progress courtesy M Hodder	Front Cover – Rose Cottage postcard courtesy B&DLHS	
77	C.Holmes up aloft courtesy S.Leighton	Back Cover Aerial view Stapleford Lane courtesy S.Leighton	
76	Sunday School Christmas Concert H. Knewstubb		
76	Coronation Hall 2009 GM	B&DLHS = Beeston & District Local History Society	
78	Invitation courtesy S. Leighton	*Every effort has been made to trace the owner of the photographs, the copyright holder. Apologies are offered for any photographs inadvertently used and on notification the matter will be rectified and specified photograph will be removed in the 2nd edition.*	
77	Whit Monday Snacks courtesy St Peter's church		
77	Whit Monday crowds courtesy E. Fletcher		
77	Site Lombardy Lodge courtesy E. Fletcher		
77	Lombardy Lodge 2012 GM		
79	Long garden, house, Nottingham Rd 2012 GM		